CSI : *HISTORY*

CONTEMPORARY
SOURCE
INVESTIGATION

Russell Rees
Andrew Blacoe
Audrey M Hodge

© Russell Rees, Andrew Blacoe and Audrey Hodge
and Colourpoint Books 2006

ISBN 13: 978 1904242 61 1
First edition
Second impression

Layout and design: Colourpoint Books
Cover design: Malcolm Johnston
Printed by: W&G Baird Ltd

Russell Rees is a practising teacher. He is
the author of *Ireland 1905–25 Vol 1: Text
and Historiography* (Colourpoint 1998) and
*Nationalism and Unionism in the Nineteenth
Century* (Colourpoint 2001), and co-author
of *Ireland, Britain and Europe from 1570–
1745*, (second edition, Colourpoint 1994)
and *Ireland and British Politics, 1870–1921*
(Colourpoint 1993). He graduated in
History with honours at the University of
Ulster and his doctoral thesis dealt with the
Northern Ireland problem between 1945
and 1951.

Andrew Blacoe is also a practising teacher.
He graduated from Queen's University,
Belfast with an Honours degree in Ancient
and Modern History and an MA in
Archaeology. He is married to Esther and
they have two children, Emma and Ben.

Audrey Hodge is also a practising teacher.
She obtained her MA in Modern and
Contemporary History at the University
of Ulster. She is the author of *Gallows
and Turnkeys* which is a short history of
Omagh Gaol, *A Congregation in the Omey*
(1997) which is a history of First Omagh
Presbyterian Church, and *The Race to Rule*
(Colourpoint 1998), as well as a series of
workbooks which accompany *Union to
Partition: Ireland 1800–1921, The Norman
Impact on the Medieval World,* and *The Race
to Rule: Ireland and Europe 1570–1700*
(Colourpoint 2006). Along with Russell
Rees, she is also the co-author of *Ireland,
Britain and Europe from 1570–1745,* and
Ireland and British Politics, 1870–1921.

Colourpoint Books
Colourpoint House
Jubilee Business Park
21 Jubilee Road
Newtownards
Co Down
BT23 4YH

Tel: 028 9182 0505
Fax: 028 9182 1900
E-mail: info@colourpoint.co.uk
Web-site: www.colourpoint.co.uk

Contents

Acknowledgements

The authors and publisher gratefully acknowledge permission to include the following copyrighted material:

Pages 9, 24 (Source 1), 43 (Source 2), 52 (Sources 1 & 2), 79 (Source 1):
Nazism 1919–1945: A Documentary Reader, Vol 1: The Rise to Power 1919–1934, edited by J Noakes and G Pridham, University of Exeter Press, new edition 1998, ISBN: 0 85989 598 X

Pages 15–16 (Source 2):
Reprinted by permission of International Creative Management Inc. Copyright © Richard Watt 1969.

Pages 25 (Source 3), 44 (Source 3):
The Coming of the Third Reich by Richard Evans (London: Penguin Books, 2003), p230. Copyright © Richard Evans 2003. Reproduced by permission of Penguin Books Ltd.

Page 35 (Source 3):
By permission of Pearson Education Limited

Page 53 (Source 3):
Hitler: 1889–1936 by Ian Kershaw (London: Allen Lane, The Penguin Press, 1998), p526. Copyright © Ian Kershaw 1998. Reproduced by permission of Penguin Books Ltd.

Page 63 (Source 3):
By permission of Philip Allan Updates

Page 71 (Source 1):
Nazism 1919–1945: A Documentary Reader, Vol 2: State, Economy and Society 1933–1939, edited by J Noakes and G Pridham, University of Exeter Press, new edition 2000, ISBN: 0 85989 599 8

Pages 71 (Source 2), 79 (Source 2), 87 (Source 1), 88 (Source 3), 95 (Source 1):
Nazism 1919–1945: A Documentary Reader, Vol 3: Foreign Policy, War and Racial Extermination, edited by J Noakes and G Pridham, University of Exeter Press, new edition 2001, ISBN: 0 85989 602 1

Page 72 (Source 3):
Reprinted by permission of John Murray

Page 96 (Source 3):
By permission of Tempus Publishing Ltd

Pages 113–114 (Source 3):
By permission of *History Ireland*. The full text of the article is available at www.historyireland.com

Page 121 (Source 1), 175 (Source 3):
By permission of Dundalgan Press

Pages 121–122 (Source 2), 137 (Source 1):
By permission of the National Library of Ireland

Pages 129–130 (Source 2):
By permission of Poolbeg Press

Page 137 (Source 2):
Extract reproduced from *The Irish Republic* by Dorothy Macardle, courtesy of Wolfhound Press, Dublin

Page 138 (Source 3):
By permission of Cambridge University Press

Pages 147 (Source 3), 155–156 (Source 2), 166 (Source 3):
By permission of Gill & Macmillan

Page 155 (Source 1):
By permission of David George Boyce

Page 156 (Source 3):
By permission of Anvil Books

Page 165 (Source 1):
From *De Valera: Long Fellow, Long Shadow* by Tim Pat Coogan, published by Hutchinson. Reprinted by permission of the Random House Group Ltd.

Page 174 (Source 1):
By permission of the Cardinal O'Fiaich Library

Pages 183–184 (Source 2):
By permission of the Ulster Historical Foundation

Page 184 (Source 3):
By permission of the Board of Trinity College, Dublin

All copyright has been acknowledged to the best of our ability. We apologise for any inadvertent omissions, which we shall endeavour to correct in any future edition.

Abbreviations

ADA   Archives of the Roman Catholic Diocese of Armagh

HC Deb   House of Commons Parliamentary Debates (Hansard)

NLI   National Library of Ireland, Dublin

TCD   Trinity College, Dublin

Introduction

ANSWERING QUESTIONS ON SOURCES

The key to successful source analysis is to ask some basic questions about the source, both in terms of its *authorship* and *content*. The aim of this section is to offer guidance on answering source questions in the AS and A2 History exam papers.

Source questions focus on *utility* and *reliability* as well as on the comparison of content.

When studying a source, and before answering a question, you should consider the following areas:

1. **AUTHOR**: Who wrote or created this source? What do you know about them and what effect may this have had on what they wrote or said? If it is a *contemporary* source, consider whether the author was there at the actual event and what his/her involvement was, and think about how this may affect their particular view of events. If the source is by a historian, think about the evidence they may have had access to and whether they have a particular historical *perspective*. Historians may also have written at different times and this affects their view of events. It may be helpful (but not crucial at AS level) to know something about the historian and his/her historical perspective, such as whether the historian is regarded as *revisionist*.

2. **DATE**: When was this source first created or written? This may mean that it is a first-hand account (*primary evidence*) but that does not necessarily mean that it is a better or more reliable source. Was the author present and writing at the time or was it written some time after the event? Did a lapse in time influence the author – may he/she have forgotten details or have been influenced by other evidence which they have heard since? Again, the date is important for a document written by a historian because new information may have become available as time passed, for example the release of Cabinet papers.

3. **CONTEXT**: While closely related to the date and the author, this is mainly concerned with what was happening around the time when the event took place or when the source was created. For example, when studying a source on Krystallnacht, you should be aware of the earlier actions of the Nazis against the Jews in Germany. You must reflect on how those events may have influenced the author. The two example analyses at the end of

this introduction illustrate what is meant by the context of the source in question.

4. **PURPOSE OR MOTIVE**: Why was the source created? What did the author hope to achieve by this information? Was this something which was just to record events privately or was it a letter or public speech which was written to persuade an audience to think in a particular way? For example, official papers are government documents and may have been intended as a means of persuading others to adopt a policy, and newspapers will usually have a clear agenda, while a diary may never have been intended for public consumption. Many newspapers are directly connected to, or even owned by, a political party and this means that they are the voice of that party, for example the *Freeman's Journal* and the IPP and *Volkischer Beobachter* and the Nazis. If the document was written by a historian who was trying to explain the events of the past, you should try to ascertain why they took that particular viewpoint. As the purpose will have affected what was actually written or created, it is therefore an important element when you examine the source for its *reliability* and *utility*.

5. **TARGET AUDIENCE**: This is clearly closely linked to the purpose of the source. Something which came from a newspaper or from a public speech will obviously have had a large and diverse audience. Equally, it is likely that this information was used in an attempt to persuade people to see things from a particular viewpoint. The people the speaker was actually addressing may not have been the sole audience for their speech, as political leaders frequently use one platform to engage with a wider audience. On the other hand, private papers or diaries have a very limited audience and may provide a more accurate picture of the author's views or feelings. They will be more *subjective* than those sources which were intended for a more public audience. However, memoirs are not similar to private papers as they are usually written for publication and sometimes to provide the author with opportunity to justify something he/she has done in the past.

6. **MODE**: You should take into account the *format* or *type* of the source. Is it from an official paper, a private paper or diary, public speeches, some aspect of the press or media, or from an informed historian's writings? Each of these formats will affect the way in which information is recorded because its purpose and target audience will differ as outlined above.

7. **TONE.** This refers to the mood which is being portrayed by the vocabulary used and, on occasions, by the sentence construction and use of punctuation, such as the frequent use of exclamation marks. You should look for words and phrases which express feelings such as anger, bitterness, disillusionment or happiness. Once again, the tone will often vary according to the mode of the source. This is because real feelings may be expressed in a private paper which will be very different in tone from a public statement by the same author, due to the difference in purpose and target audience.

8. **CONTENT**: This will of course differ depending on all of the factors outlined above. In any question which asks about the content, all other factors should be explored first.

QUESTIONS FOCUSING ON UTILITY

In both AS and A2 papers, questions are asked about *utility* ("How useful is this source to a historian studying …?")

As a general rule, all sources will be useful for something, otherwise they would not appear on an examination paper. Read the question carefully, paying particular attention to the direction given by the examiner. For example, if you are asked about a source's usefulness in relation to the treatment of women in Nazi Germany, keep this as your focus throughout your answer. Make use of all the factors mentioned, for example check dates (remember that a source written in 1930 about Nazi election success will be of limited use to a historian studying Nazi success in the period 1930–33).

You must ask how is the source useful in answering the specific question – what does it tell me, who is the author, when, why, how, and for whom? Comment should be made on the effect of these factors on the source's utility.

You must also examine the limitations of each source in answering the specific question – what does it *not* tell me, what other viewpoints are missing, how is it influenced by its context? Does a historian need information from a different period, from a different mode, and for a different audience to enable him/her to get a fuller picture?

 THERE SHOULD ALWAYS BE POINTS TO SUPPORT THE UTILITY OF A SOURCE AND OTHER POINTS WHICH ILLUSTRATE ITS LIMITATIONS.

QUESTIONS FOCUSING ON COMPARISON OF CONTENT

When answering a question about how and why two sources differ, you should identify all the ways in which the content differs by carefully reading each source and underlining or highlighting the main points made and then marking out the points on which they agree and disagree. This will form the basis of your answer.

If the sources come from different viewpoints, written perhaps at different times for different audiences, then this will help you explain why they differ. The mode and tone should also be compared. It is not a good idea simply to state that sources are biased.

USING THIS BOOK

The AS section sets out sample answers in note form, to offer students an introduction to approaching source questions, while the A2 section gives full sample essays for each question.

When answering AS questions on *usefulness* and *how and why*, technique is vital. The various areas of Date, Author, Mode, etc must each be explored in order to fully exploit each of the sources. However, the order in which these areas are addressed in this book (for both Questions 1 and 2) is in no way intended to be definitive, but is rather one suggested approach. To gain maximum marks in *usefulness* questions, the usefulness of the source must be balanced with its *limitations*. Likewise, in *how and why* questions the motive must be discussed.

SAMPLE SOURCE ANALYSIS: THE NAZIS AND GERMANY 1919–1945

If the man's world is said to be the State, his struggle, his readiness to devote his powers to the service of the community, then it may perhaps be said that the woman's is a smaller world. For her world is her husband, her family, her children, and her home. But what would become of the greater world if there were no one to tend and care for the smaller one? How could the greater world survive if there were no one to make the cares of the smaller world the content of their lives? No, the greater world is built on the foundation of this smaller world. This great world cannot survive if the smaller world is not stable. Providence has entrusted to the woman the cares of that world which is her very own, and only on the basis of this smaller world can the man's world be formed and built up. The two worlds are not antagonistic. They complement each other, they belong together just as man and woman belong together.

Extract from Hitler's speech to the National Socialist Women's section (NSF), 8 September 1934, elaborating on the official Nazi attitude to women
J Noakes and G Pridham (eds), *Nazism 1919–1945, vol 2*
(University of Exeter Press, 2000)

Q

Study Source 1. How useful is it as evidence for a historian studying Nazi attitudes towards women in the period 1933–39?

Usefulness for the study of women	
Date/Context	During the 'liberal' days of Weimar, the emancipation of women had (in theory at least) not only provided them with a vote but also equal status with men. Nazi 'anti-feminism' was largely a reaction to this, but this is not to say that the Nazis were out of touch with social thinking of the period. While extreme, a similar outlook to that of the Nazis could be found in large sections of the rural community, and was supported by the churches and some political parties before 1933.
	The Nazis believed that men and women were naturally different and had distinct roles to play, the women's being in the home and the raising of children. They also were not to have a role in the hierarchy of politics. Women were not inferior, just different.

	8 September 1934 – This speech is extremely useful in that it is just after Hitler has consolidated his power by receiving the personal oath of loyalty from the army after the death of Hindenburg.
Author	Hitler
Mode	Speech
Target audience	National Socialist Women's section (NSF)
Tone/ Language	The source is not 'dictatorial' in tone. While key ideology is expressed about a woman's role, words such as "tend", "care" and "complement" are 'soft' and understanding. Hitler is not trying to push his ideas on women, but rather persuade them, making this source not only useful for understanding attitudes towards women but also as an example of Nazi propaganda.
Content	A woman's role is summed up by the line "For her world is her husband, her family, her children, and her home." Women are to be the stable foundation of man's "greater world", with "Providence" entrusting them to the care of their "smaller world". The source finishes on an 'equality' theme, in that the two worlds of both man and woman should complement each other.
Motive/ Purpose	While this source gives us a so-called official Nazi attitude towards women, it is far from being the true belief of Hitler. In reality, Hitler viewed women as being servants of men, not their equals. A woman's place was in the home and, more importantly, a woman's duty was to provide many, healthy and pure children for the state. This source, while being close to Hitler's final consolidation of power in August 1934, was probably an attempt to win over the female population of Germany. The topic of the role of the sexes was, and still is, a very difficult one to discuss, especially at government level. This can be illustrated by Hitler's obvious caution and careful wording while speaking to women already enrolled in a Nazi organisation.

	While the source gives us the official view of Nazi attitudes to women, there are some limitations to its content, as hinted at previously.
	◆ There is no discussion of any specific Nazi policy towards women in Germany. As with any group discussed in Nazi Germany, we can identify attitudes and ideology by studying the policies made by Hitler. This source has none, eg Marriage Loan or Marriage Law, the limitations of enrolment for university, or the dismissal of women from top civil service jobs.
Limitations	◆ While the speech talks of marriage, the Nazis introduced the Lebensborn programme which encouraged births outside marriage.
	◆ The speech mentions a woman being at home, which contradicts later Nazi policy, eg 1939 Compulsory Agricultural Labour Service for unmarried women under 25.
	Any discussion of Nazi attitudes towards women have to take into account the changing role of women throughout the whole period. While useful, this source has obvious limitations and lacks specific Nazi policies.

SAMPLE SOURCE ANALYSIS: THE PARTITION OF IRELAND 1900–1925

I admit they were wrong; I know they were wrong; but they fought a clean fight, and they fought with superb bravery and skill, and no act … against the usual custom of war … has been brought home to any leader …

As a matter of fact, the great bulk of the population were not favourable to the insurrection, and the insurgents themselves, who had confidently counted on a rising of the people in their support, were absolutely disappointed.

They got no popular support whatsoever. What is happening is that thousands of people in Dublin, who ten days ago were bitterly opposed to the whole Sinn Fein movement and to the rebellion, are now becoming infuriated against the Government on account of these executions and, as I am informed by letters received this morning, that feeling is spreading throughout the country in a most dangerous degree …

We who speak for the vast majority of the Irish people, we who have risked a great deal to win the people to your side in this great crisis of your Empire's history, we who have … successfully endeavoured to secure that the Irish in America shall not go into alliance with the Germans in that country – we, I think, were entitled to be consulted before this bloody course of executions was entered upon in Ireland.

Extract from a speech by MP John Dillon in the House of Commons, 11 May 1916
HC Deb 5th Series, vol 82

The timing of John Dillon's speech in the House of Commons is very significant. Delivered on 11 May 1916, just after the Rising and during the ten-day period of executions which ran from 3 to 12 May, Dillon provides a contemporary view of the impact that the British policy of executions was having on Nationalist Ireland. In the speech Dillon presses Herbert Asquith, the Prime Minister, for an assurance that the executions would end, but none was forthcoming. The Easter Rising had begun on Monday 24 April and fighting continued until Sunday 1 May. The British Army had used artillery to attack the insurgents who had occupied important buildings close to Dublin's city centre. Over 200 civilians had died in the fighting and damage to property was estimated at £3,000,000. Martial law was imposed over the whole country and the leaders of the rebellion were tried by secret courts martial. Executions began on 3 May and continued intermittently until 12 May when James Connolly and Sean MacDermott faced the firing squad. Accordingly, as

Dillon rose to speak in the House of Commons, he had no indication that the next day would mark the end of the executions and instead assumed that middle-ranking rebel leaders would also be executed.

Of course, Dillon's credentials as a spokesman for Nationalist Ireland were impeccable. He was the grandson of John Blake Dillon, the Young Irelander, and had first been elected to Westminster in 1880. Dillon had also served as one of Parnell's chief lieutenants, and he had been the number two figure in the IPP behind John Redmond since 1900. A staunch supporter of the Liberal alliance, Dillon was not always comfortable with Redmond's leadership, and their differences became more discernible after the outbreak of the First World War. While Redmond had responded with enthusiasm to the call to arms and had thrown himself into the recruitment campaign in Ireland, Dillon had maintained a lofty detachment, refusing to appear on any recruiting platform. At Westminster, therefore, it was no surprise that his brand of Irish Nationalism was viewed as more militant than Redmond's by MPs on the mainland.

Another crucial factor determining the importance of the Dillon speech is that he, alone of the IPP leadership, was in Dublin for the duration of the Rising and had therefore an eyewitness view of events as they developed. While Redmond remained in London, Dillon was trapped in his house close to O'Connell Street (Sackville Street), but by the end of the fighting he was in a position to gauge reaction on the streets. In his speech Dillon confirms the conventional view that the initial reaction to the insurgents was hostile. Of course, this view has recently been challenged by a number of historians, notably Joe Lee, who have argued that early reaction in the provinces to the news of the rebellion was broadly sympathetic to the insurgents' actions, once it became clear that the Rising was neither a German-led plot nor a Bolshevik-type coup. From his vantage point in Dublin, however, Dillon emphasises that the Rising had failed dismally to attract popular support, but the speech also records his view that opinion was shifting. Indeed, he had written to Redmond on 7 May 1916 warning that Dublin residents, who had no sympathy with the insurgents, were becoming increasingly bitter about the British response.

Clearly, the tone of the speech is angry and bitter. Dillon denounces the executions, and although he deplores their actions he praises the moral courage of the participants. In another part of the speech he made reference to the Sheehy-Skeffington murder which had undoubtedly inflamed the situation in Dublin and helped to turn the tide against the British. In this sense Dillon is providing an accurate commentary on the impact of the Dublin rumour mill at the time, as executions were carried out in secrecy without any consultation with the immediate families of the victims. Stories circulating about the last hours of the condemned men and the perception of "blood seeping beneath a closed door" with no end in sight to the executions were clearly having a profound effect on Nationalist opinion. Dillon's speech, therefore, is crucial as it presents a first-hand account of the sea change in Nationalist politics caused by reaction in Ireland to the executions. Moreover, the bitterness of Dillon's denunciation of British policy and his condemnation of the military authorities' unrestrained brutality caught the House of Commons by surprise and outraged Tory backbenchers.

However, the Dillon speech does more than simply analyse the impact of the executions on the Irish Nationalist psyche. Dillon has an ulterior motive. His target audience is not just the assembled MPs in the Commons but Nationalist voters in Ireland. A clear purpose of the speech is a desperate attempt to halt the drift in support from the IPP to Sinn Féin. His frustration with British insensitivity and short-sightedness has turned to anger as he sees the British "manufacturing Sinn Féiners" in huge numbers. The great strength of this source is that it offers a powerful analysis of the transformation that took place at this point in the Irish revolution. The biggest casualty of Easter 1916 was constitutional Nationalism, and in spite of Dillon's heroic attempt to shore up the IPP's defences it was quickly apparent that the Rising had cruelly exposed the party's limitations. Moreover, Dillon could see this more clearly than Redmond. To an extent the speech can be regarded as an echo of Parnellism, as Dillon tries to claim the militants as his own and steer his party down a more militant road that would incorporate the decisive shift in Nationalist opinion. After all, Dillon fully understood that it was Parnell's brand of militant constitutionalism that made his party the powerful movement that it was in the 1880s. However, Dillon's dramatic intervention proved futile. Redmond rejected any bold initiative and instead opted for negotiations with Lloyd George, further compromise, and ultimately – as his Sinn Féin opponents chided him – humiliation.

Dillon could see his own life's work and all the efforts of his party being cast aside at this crucial moment, and this explains his reference to the risks being taken by the IPP. Irish Nationalists had supported the war effort and they had used their considerable influence in America to promote a pro-British line among that country's Irish population. Yet the party's contribution to the peaceful solution of the Irish Question was now, in Dillon's view, being wasted by actions carried out in the name of the British government.

Overall, this source is of great value for any historian looking at the transformation of Nationalist Ireland after the Rising, and it is a vital document in explaining the rapid decline of the IPP which culminated in the Sinn Féin general election landslide of December 1918.

AS: The Nazis and Germany 1919–1945

GERMAN REVOLUTION

Source 1

The old foundations of the German position based on force are forever destroyed. The Prussian hegemony, the Hohenzollern army, the policy of the shining armour have been made impossible among us for all future. As November 9, 1918, follows on March 18, 1848, so must we here in Weimar complete the change from Imperialism to Idealism, from world power to spiritual greatness. ("Hear, hear.")

… So will we set to work with our great goal clear before our eyes. To maintain the right of the German people, to anchor firmly in Germany a strong democracy and to fill it with true social spirit and Socialist character. ("Hear, hear.")

So shall we create an Empire of right and of righteousness, founded on the equality of everything that wears the form of mankind.

Extract from President Ebert's Address to the Opening Session of the German Assembly, 7 February 1919
Source Records of the Great War, **vol VII, ed Charles Horne (National Alumni, 1923)**

Source 2

They [Karl Liebknecht and Rosa Luxemburg] were taken to headquarters in the Eden Hotel for questioning, in the course of which they were beaten. Later in the night … Liebknecht and Luxemburg were brought out separately As Liebknecht emerged … an enormously built private … raised his rifle and smashed it down on Liebknecht's head …

A few moments later Rosa Luxemburg hobbled out … She too was clubbed with [the] rifle … [Liebknecht] was shot twice while 'attempting to escape'.

> *No one knows whether Rosa Luxemburg was still alive when Lieutenant Vogel blew out her brains with a single shot.*
>
> **From Richard M Watt, *The Kings Depart: The Tragedy of Germany: Versailles and the German Revolution* (Weidenfeld & Nicolson, 1969) Watt reconstructs the murder of Karl Liebknecht and Rosa Luxemburg by the government-backed Free Corps.**

Source 3

The alliance of 1918 between the moderate army leaders and the moderate Socialist leaders against the – real or imagined – threat of Bolshevism and chaos ensured a large degree of continuity with the past. The Kaiser and the other monarchs abdicated, but the States they had ruled, together with the bureaucracies [ie governments] of those States, survived. The nucleus [ie core] of the old Prussian army survived, and soon hardly bothered to conceal its contempt [ie dislike] for the party politicians who held office ... Women were given the vote, and the parties changed their names to accord with the 'democratic' spirit of the times, but their attitudes remained conditioned by their experiences under the old régime. There was, then, a break in continuity in 1918, but that break was superficial, and it was only a question of time before the old forces began to reassert themselves.

From John Charles Gerald Röhl, *From Bismarck to Hitler: The Problems of Continuity in German History* (Longmans, 1970)

Q1

Study Source 1. How useful is it as evidence for a historian studying the German Revolution of 1918–19?

Usefulness for the study of the German Revolution	
Date/Context	The German Revolution began on 10 November 1918 when Kaiser Wilhelm II, having abdicated, left for Holland. On 11 November representatives of the new German 'government' signed the armistice with the allies. With unrest in Berlin reaching a peak during the Spartacist Revolution of January 1919, discussions for the new constitution of Germany were finalised in Weimar. This address to the opening session of

	the German Assembly on 7 February 1919 comes in the wake of this extreme political violence, making Ebert's comments regarding the future path of German politics very striking indeed.
Author	President Ebert in essence represented the German Revolution of 1918–19. He had become its chief representative and should therefore understand its aims and objectives better than anyone else. This opening speech gives us these aims straight from the top.
Mode/ Target audience	Still in its infancy, this speech is declaring a new future for Germany – a new beginning. While it is being delivered to the German Assembly, there is no doubt that it would have been reported in the press the following day, thereby making it a speech to the German people as well.
Tone/ Language	The tone of the speech can be found in statements like "… based on force are forever destroyed", "So will we set to work …" and "So shall we create …" This speech has a sense of defiance and confidence, with Ebert clearly taking charge and laying a new path for Germany. This makes the source useful for a historian studying the Revolution in light of the violent events of previous weeks.
Content	The source opens with "The old foundations of the German position based on force are forever destroyed", a claim that is backed up in the following statement condemning the military influence of Prussia. What is desired is "Idealism" and "spiritual greatness". These are interesting comments considering Ebert's position in February 1919, having led the country with no political mandate since 9 November 1918, but rather through the army, Free Corps and General Groener. The speech could be taken at face value and be regarded as a change of heart, a desire to right the wrongs of, for example, the measures taken against Rosa Luxemburg and Karl Liebknecht. This, as we know, did not happen and subsequent left-wing revolutions were dealt with in the old 'Prussian', forceful way.
	The second section of the source seems to reflect the first in its idealism, with its desire for a "strong democracy" and a "true social spirit". The "Socialist character" however did not

	include the KPD, the German Communist party (the name taken by the Spartacists before the January Revolution). This seems ironic considering the final line of the source and the founding of an Empire "on the equality of everything". Equality therefore was only applicable to those the socialists chose.
Motive/ Purpose	Ebert's control of Germany had been nothing short of weak from the outset. Based on nothing more than a secret deal with General Groener, Ebert had compromised democracy for the maintenance of power. The speech could represent a genuine desire for democracy to take precedence, a desire to move towards a more embracing political culture. Ebert was a democrat from before the war, possessing in 1918 a clear vision for a new, decisive Reichstag unlike that under the Kaiser. Ebert's dream of democracy had become a reality through the Revolution of late 1918. It had not been planned or orchestrated by him, nor had he been an active participant in the declaration of a republic, but Ebert had embraced the role of 'president-elect' given to him and did not intend to let it go. The deal with Groener was based on a mutual dislike of the Communists. Both men saw them as a potential root cause of Germany's downfall. The army and the elite were fearful of losing their privileged status and class, and Ebert was fearful of losing political control to a soviet-styled government. Democracy could only work if the Communists were curtailed, a task that Groener was only too glad to undertake. In this light it could be said that in the turbulent and uncertain days of November 1918, Ebert's deal was understandable, if not necessary, for Germany to remain 'soviet-free'. The source must therefore be a reflection of Ebert's true intentions for the new Germany, a vision which he had held and perfected for many years. It must also be remembered that Ebert was a politician. His desire for the 'old' elite ways to be removed was shared by the majority of Germans who, at least in February 1919, saw democracy as the new way forward from the dark days of

	autocratic rule under the Kaiser. In his manifesto of January 1919, Ebert had promised freedoms beyond that of any nation in the world. This address confirms those promises.
Limitations	• There is no mention of the Groener deal which characterised the revolution from 9 November 1918 to 1919 and beyond. • There is no discussion of Communism and how it would be dealt with in the future. Looking at the source in isolation, it could give the impression that Ebert had never used force in the past and would never use it in the future, but we know this to be false. • It also fails to give us the reasons for the onset of the German Revolution, including such details as the abdication of the king. • The speech is obviously a propaganda message and needs to be read with a degree of caution.

Q2

Sources 1 and 2 provide different accounts of the German Revolution of 1918–19. How and why do they differ?

How		
Themes	**Source 1**	**Source 2**
Date/Context	7 February 1919, Opening Session of new German Assembly	1969
Author	President Ebert	Richard M Watt
Mode	Address/Speech	Book
Target audience	German Assembly/general public	General public
Tone/Language	Confident and clear, determined	Dramatic style, using phrases like "smashed it down" and "clubbed with rifle"

Content	• Old Germany based on force is gone • Change from Imperialism to Idealism • Maintenance of right of German people • Strong democracy • Creation of Empire of right and righteousness, founded on equality	• Liebknecht and Luxemburg taken in for questioning and beaten • Later brought out and Liebknecht has head smashed with rifle butt • Luxemburg also clubbed with rifle • Liebknecht shot twice while attempting to escape • Luxemburg shot in head

Why		
Themes	**Source 1**	**Source 2**
Context	**Basic difference overview** Government pledge that violent days of old Germany are over **Context** • Ebert has been in power since 10 November with the abdication of Kaiser Wilhelm II. He has no real political authority. Instead, authority rests on a secret deal made with General Groener, who promised the army would defend the new government in return for a government promise to maintain the authority of existing army officers.	**Basic difference overview** Government use of violence to maintain power and destroy threats **Context** • Written well after the event, there should be no underlying motives in this source which could influence its quality or usefulness.

	• From the signing of the armistice, Ebert's authority and the new system of government has been challenged by other political parties in Germany and extremist groups.	
Motive/ Purpose	• Need for calm after the violence of early January when the Spartacists (renamed German Communist Party) attempted to seize power via armed revolution • Genuine desire to implement socialist ideals and defend them against Communist attacks (Communism being seen by the Social Democratic Party as an enemy as much as the Right) • Genuine desire to establish a strong democracy after the authoritarian rule of the Kaiser • Ebert's use of the Free Corps to end the left-wing violence would have been widely publicised, perhaps influencing this speech and its desire to wipe the slate clean.	• Author wanted to make money from the sale of book • Author interested in topic and wanted to show the ruthlessness of the Free Corps in doing the work of the government • Could have Communist sympathies in light of ongoing Cold War

Q3

Using the sources *and* your own knowledge, assess the success of the Revolution in Germany in establishing a strong foundation for democracy.

What was the German Revolution?

Beginning in September 1918 and ending in February the following year, the German Revolution saw Germany's system of government change from a monarchy to a democratic republic.

Key Themes	Date	Event
Revolution from above	29 September 1918	Generals recommend a new civilian government and an armistice.
	2 October 1918	General Ludendorff addresses the Reichstag and announces "we cannot win this war".
	3 October 1918	Prince Max of Baden heads new civilian government based on Reichstag support.
Revolution from below	31 October 1918	Mutiny at Kiel that spreads to surrounding ports and then inland. Soldiers', sailors', and workers' councils established.
	9 November 1918	Prince Max steps down and Ebert (unwillingly) becomes chancellor. Philip Scheidemann (Leader of the SPD) declares a republic and the Kaiser abdicates, leaving for Holland.
Limited Revolution	10 November 1918	Ebert makes secret deal with General Groener – the army will protect and support the new government in return for the maintenance of the authority of existing officers.
Armistice	11 November 1918	New government signs armistice with the allies in the Foret de Compiegne.
Revolution slows	December 1918	The National Congress of Workers' and Soldiers' Councils vote 344 to 98 to reject a government based on councils, preferring Ebert's first choice for a constituent assembly.

Revolution stops	January 1919	Hardline socialists, still unhappy at Ebert's moderate line, protest at a radical official's dismissal, resulting in a spontaneous uprising led by the German Communist Party (formerly called the Spartacist League). Both Karl Liebknecht and Rosa Luxemburg shot, along with over 100 workers, by government troops supported by the Freikorps.
New system established	February 1919	Government move from violence of Berlin to quiet city of Weimar where constitution is drafted (although not formalised until August).

The Revolution was limited in many ways (Source 3). Ebert's choices were limited in themselves as the nature of his authority was not democratic until February the following year. Ebert's 'necessary' deal with Groener to stop the spread of Bolshevism was genuine enough, but it was to have extreme consequences later in the life of the republic. This deal kept the army and the elite in the seat of power, albeit secretly, from 1918 to 1919, but with the 1925 presidential election and the appointment of Paul von Hindenburg the army/elite were back in control. This, as we know, would be fatal for the republic and would result in the appointment of Hitler into the position of chancellor in January 1933.

Ebert's use of extreme violence, as seen in Source 2, was not a reflection of his true nature, unlike Defence Minister Gustav Noske who was in charge of the army and Freikorps. Ebert's true passion was socialism and democracy (Source 1), but it was these very qualities that denied him the respect of the large majority of ordinary Germans who had no experience of 'people power'.

Perhaps Ebert's worst decision was to have the most open and liberal constitution the world had ever seen. Having maintained power from November 1918 to February 1919 using the army, Ebert's desire to protect socialism and democracy with Article 48 (Emergency Powers for the President) opened the door for a dictator. Ebert's 'inclusive politics' brought about a proportional representation electoral system that resulted in continual Coalition governments and weak democracy. Combined with Ebert's use of violence, using the Freikorps set a precedent for violence to be used against the government in return. Ebert's destruction of the Left and leniency towards the Right (because of his siding with the elite and army) allowed extremism and hatred to grow unchecked in the mid-1920s.

Born out of defeat, aided with violence and with a failure to understand the true desires of the elite, Ebert's genuine efforts to establish democracy gained only a facade of approval from those people who were asked to make it work but who actually sought to bring it to its knees.

23

Munich Putsch and its significance

Source 1

The column of National Socialists about 2,000 strong, nearly all armed, moved on through ... The police used rubber truncheons and rifle butts and tried to push back the crowd with rifles held horizontally ... Suddenly, a National Socialist fired a pistol at a police officer from close quarters. The shot ... killed Sergeant Hollweg ... Even before it was possible to give an order, the comrades of the sergeant ... opened fire as the Hitler lot did, and a short gun battle ensued ... After no more than thirty seconds the Hitler lot fled ...

Extract from the official report prepared for the committee of inquiry following the Munich Putsch in 1924
J Noakes and G Pridham (eds), *Nazism 1919–1945, vol 1*
(University of Exeter Press, 1998)

Source 2

I [Ludecke] noticed that he [Hitler] barred in particular any reminder of the putsch ...

'From now on,' he said, 'we must follow a new line of action. It is best to attempt no large reorganisation until I am freed, which may be a matter of months rather than years.'

...'Oh yes', he continued, '... When I resume active work it will be necessary to pursue a new policy. Instead of working to achieve power by armed conspiracy, we shall have to hold our noses and enter the Reichstag against the Catholic and Marxist deputies. If outvoting them takes longer than outshooting them, at least the results will be guaranteed by their own Constitution! ... Sooner or later we shall have a majority, and after that we shall have Germany.

Extract from a conversation between Kurt Ludecke, a Nazi associate, and Hitler, while the latter was in Landsberg Prison, 1924
Kurt W Ludecke, *I Knew Hitler* (Jarrolds, 1938)

Source 3

By 1929 Hitler had attracted the support, sympathy and to some extent even the financial backing of some well-connected people, especially in Bavaria. And his movement had extended its operations across the whole country, attracting significant electoral support, above all among crisis-racked small farmers in Protestant areas of north Germany and Franconia.

None of this could disguise the fact, however, that in the autumn of 1929, the Nazi Party was still very much on the fringes of politics ... The Republic seemed to have weathered the storms of the early 1920s – the inflation, the French occupation, the armed conflicts ... and to have entered calmer waters. It would need a catastrophe of major dimensions if an extremist party like the Nazis was to gain mass support.

From Richard J Evans, *The Coming of the Third Reich* (Penguin Books, 2003)

Q1

Study Source 1. How useful is it as evidence for a historian studying the Munich Putsch in November 1923?

Usefulness for the study of the Munich Putsch	
Date/Context	With inflation already rising at the beginning of 1923, Germany's failure to pay its second instalment of reparations in 1922 led to the invasion of the Ruhr by the French and Belgian armies and the subsequent hyperinflation crisis. While some individuals gained from the financial problems, eg Hugo Stinnes, most of the peasant and middle classes lost whatever savings they had. As the situation grew worse, democracy itself came under constant pressure from both Left and Right to find a solution. The latter came in the form of Gustav Stresemann who, having been appointed chancellor in August, called off passive resistance, stopped the printing of money, and established (under the leadership of Hjlamar Schacht) the Rentenmark. By November the worst of the hyperinflation crisis was over, but this did not prevent the Nazis from making an attempt at seizing power.

	Hitler's actions were not simply conditioned by the financial pressures of late 1923. The leadership of Bavaria headed by Gustav von Kahr had, in principle, decided on a military coup on Berlin to take power for themselves. This decision probably came as a direct result of rumours of another attempt on power by a right wing group called the Kampfbund. This group, made up of a variety of right wing fascist-style parties including the Nazis and the SA, had decided that their coup would take place on 12 November. Hitler, a leading member of the executive committee of the Kampfbund, knew that if the Nazis were to make their mark they had to act alone. Von Kahr had scheduled a meeting of interest for his attempt on power on 8 November in the Burgerbraukeller. It was this meeting that Hitler and the SA would storm, recruit the three state leaders of Bavaria, and lead the assault on Berlin – Ebert's democracy. Produced in 1924, the report is highly useful for the study of the Putsch. A contemporary document, we can see how the Nazi attempt to seize power was 'reported' at the time with the information available. Referring to 9 November, we read the official version of the failed attempt to march through Munich and rally support for the Putsch.
Author	As an official report, it is likely that this evidence was compiled from a variety of eyewitness accounts including bystanders and police. Most importantly though, this account or report is *for* and *by* the government and therefore lets us see just what evidence was levelled against Hitler and the Nazis in the courtroom.
Mode	As a report, the source is invaluable from the point of view of the government's prosecution of major criminals accused of treason. The report should contain the main facts relating to the Putsch and the role of the Nazis, as it would have been used as evidence in Hitler's trial for treason.
Target audience	The target audience for this source is not just the Committee of Inquiry. Prosecution lawyers would have used this evidence during Hitler's trial and, via the press, this would have been relayed to the general public.

Tone/ Language	While an official report, the language appears to be quite dramatic, using words and phrases such as "Suddenly" and "Even before it was possible". This suggests that the report was deliberately enhanced to present the Nazis in a particularly bad light.
Content	The content is useful as it gives us specific details of the number of Nazis taking part ("2,000"), their level of preparedness ("nearly all armed"), and the actions taken by the police to stop them. From the account it is clear who the report blames for the deaths at the end of the Putsch. It states "Suddenly, a National Socialist fired a pistol at a police officer from close quarters" and that the officer's "comrades" defended themselves. The end of the report indicates that "the Hitler lot fled", perhaps inferring cowardice on the part of the Nazis.
Motive/ Purpose	The purpose of the source, as a report for the committee of inquiry, should have been to provide a factual account of the Putsch for the use of the state prosecution in the trial of Hitler and the Nazi Party. The use of emotive language and contentious information, like the Nazis opening fire first or the Hitler lot fleeing, suggest the source is not as balanced as it could be. The motive behind this report may simply be to paint the picture of an organised, violent Nazi putsch, and a heroic victory for the policemen who bravely stood against the Nazis and won.
Limitations	As suggested above, the source does have its problems. • Some historians put the figure of Nazis moving through the streets at 3,000, not 2,000, and most would agree that less than half were armed. • It is also unlikely that the Munich police would have turned up at a barricade to face the Nazis and SA with rubber truncheons, as we know that it was Gustav von Kahr who mobilised them after being held captive in the Burgerbraukeller the night before. • The source fails to mention the previous evening (8 November in the beer hall) at all and thereby misses the reason for the march on the centre of Munich the following day. • The source also lacks the reason for the Nazis attempting a putsch in the first place.

The source is useful to a point. It does give us a government perspective on the Putsch on 9 November and allows us to see bias in government documents. However, the source does not provide any reasons for the Putsch itself and has no information on 8 November and the beer hall. While a useful document in itself, this source would need to be balanced with a Nazi perspective.

Q2

Sources 1 and 2 provide different contemporary accounts of methods used by the Nazis to gain power in Weimar Germany. *How* and *why* do they differ?

How		
Themes	**Source 1**	**Source 2**
Date/Context	1924	1924
Author	Civil servants	Kurt Ludecke, former Nazi associate of Hitler
Mode	Official report	Conversation reproduced in book
Target audience	Committee of inquiry	General public
Tone/Language	Reporting style, although some glimpses of narrative with "suddenly" and "comrades"	Confident tone, clear vision of future – "we shall have Germany"
Content	• Putsch of 2,000 SA marching through street • Police stop flow through streets • SA open fire and gun battle ensues	• Hitler says new line of action to be taken to gain power after he is released from prison • Armed coups to be forgotten and replaced by politics

	• Hitler lot flees • Attempt to take over power by force is failure	• Nazi Party to use the constitution (legal methods) to gain power • Primary goal a parliamentary majority

Why		
Themes	**Source 1**	**Source 2**
Context	**Basic difference overview** Hitler's failed attempt to take power by force **Context** • Hitler's Munich Putsch between 8–9 November had been an attempt to seize power in the state and then 'March on Berlin'. Looking objectively at the timing of the event, it could be suggested that there wasn't a better time to attempt a putsch: Germany had suffered a humiliating hyperinflation crisis and the government had given in to the French and ended passive resistance. The reality was somewhat different in that Hitler feared that either the Kampfbund (a grouping of extremist right wing paramilitaries, including the SA) or the leaders of Bavaria themselves would beat him and the Nazis to it.	**Basic difference overview** Hitler's change of tactics in the pursuit of power from violence to politics **Context** • Hitler's imprisonment in Landsberg prison was lenient. Landsberg was not maximum security and Hitler enjoyed many visitations and received countless letters during his time there. There have been claims that some guards gave the fascist salute and called Hitler "Führer". • During his imprisonment, Hitler's initial thoughts that Ludendorff would lead Germany after the successful Putsch faded. Hitler began to see himself as Germany's saviour and to think that he alone would make all decisions regarding the Nazi Party's future (Führerprinzip).

	• The Putsch was planned on the night of 7 November.	• Hitler also wrote *Mein Kampf* ('My Struggle') with the help of Max Amman and Rudolf Hess.
Motive/ Purpose	• The report was probably made to lay full blame at the feet of Hitler and the Nazis. • There has always been controversy as to who opened fire first – the police or the Nazis. This report leaves no doubt. • The report would obviously wish to paint the authorities in a better light than the Nazis.	• Kurt Ludecke became a former Nazi associate in the early 1930s. Published later in the decade, *I Knew Hitler* became a bestseller. • Ludecke may have wished to claim to be the first person to hear Hitler's dramatic pronouncement of an end to violence and a move towards politics. This would thereby elevate Ludecke to a position of great importance in the reader's mind. • Ludecke possibly wished to portray Hitler as some type of visionary/prophet who saw his rise to power years before it actually occurred.

Q3

Using the sources *and* your own knowledge, assess the significance of the Munich Putsch for the political fortunes of the Nazi Party in the period 1924–29.

What was the Munich Putsch?

Against the backdrop of countless revolutions and violence, anger at the government for signing the Treaty of Versailles, and huge economic trauma suffered during the hyperinflation crisis, the Nazi Party and its leader Adolf Hitler sought to gain power in Bavaria by force and then, like Mussolini's 'March on Rome', march to Berlin and seize the government of Germany.

This grand plan never stood a chance and Hitler knew it. So why did he continue? The answer was simple. The Nazi Party, and Hitler, were well known inside Bavaria for being right wing extremists but outside the state they were nothing but agitators at best. Bavaria had been the seat of right wing dissent against Versailles since May 1919, after the destruction of the Soviet-style republic. Organised like a dictatorship by state commissioner Gustav von Kahr with the help of Otto von Lossow (commander of the Reichswehr), the Bavarian government had considered a 'March on Berlin' themselves but had feared defeat. Hitler knew of these plans, and those of the Kampfbund – a group of right wing activists who were planning the same action for 12 November. Hitler, while part of the Kampfbund (the SA formed the largest part of the organisation), knew that if the Nazi Party and he were to ever gain power it should be as themselves and not as part of something else. This desire for exclusivity and the narrow time frame for action pushed Hitler into the Putsch sooner than desired. Having met secretly with the Chief of Police on 7 November and been told there would be no support for any uprising, Hitler proceeded on 8 November anyway.

Countless errors were made on the night, the most important being General Ludendorff's decision to let von Kahr and von Lossow leave (under a 'gentleman's oath' to carry out their promises to begin the revolution!) the Burgerbraukeller beer hall, whereupon they set out to stop the Nazis and retain their power in the state. In effect, the Putsch was over as the two leaders of the government set about raising the police and army against the rising. The second mistake was for Hitler to listen to the advice of Ludendorff to march through the streets of Munich and rally support from the public. At noon on 9 November, the Nazis moved through the streets (Source 1), only to find not support but opposition. The Putsch ended in a gun battle and defeat and, after being removed from the scene in a taxi, Hitler was subsequently arrested two days later on 11 November.

The trial

It was at Hitler's 'show' trial that the Nazi Party gained its victory, for Hitler won his notoriety through hours of speeches (allowed by the court) and reports printed in national newspapers. Hitler became a national figure. His lenient sentence at Landsberg Fortress provided the stage for an even bigger victory, at least in the mind of Hitler himself. While in prison Hitler found his personal destiny – he alone would be the saviour of Germany and he alone would lead it. The Nazi Party would change and seek power through different means (Source 2), and the party's structure would meet this new challenge with Hitler as sole leader and decider of policy (the Führerprinzip). Perhaps most importantly, Hitler wrote *Mein Kampf* ('My Struggle'). Nazi ideology, its aims and objectives, its likes and dislikes, and its leader's innermost thoughts on all aspects of life were all captured on paper. While rambling in style, this document provided Hitler with his sense of purpose. It cleared his vision.

Reformation?

After Hitler's release in December 1924 and re-founding of the party in February 1925 along the Führerprinzip, the Nazi Party failed to make an electoral impact. Why? The propaganda was essentially the same as that of the early 1930s which made them into the largest party in the Reichstag. The street rallies were as powerful and colourful as would have been expected and Hitler was still an excellent speaker, but by the 1928 Reichstag elections the Nazis had gained only 12 seats – just 2.7% of the vote.

Realities

The Nazi Party of 1925–28 was competing in a very different political and economic climate to that of 1929–33. Weimar, at least on the surface, was experiencing a type of prosperity, if only on borrowed money. This feel-good factor allowed democracy to exist, indeed it gave it a second chance after the shame of Versailles and the nightmare of hyperinflation. While many of the organisations of the Nazi Party were formed after, and as a result of, the Putsch (eg the Hitler Youth, Nazi Teachers' League), Hitler's personal control of the party was not secure until after the Bamberg conference of 1926, when all local offices of the party met and agreed the previously made 25-point programme, as well as Hitler's sole control. The Nazis were therefore in no real position to contest any elections by 1928.

Failure?

By 1929 the Nazis were politically nowhere. It would need a miracle to take power (Source 3). That came in October in 1929 with the collapse of Wall Street in America and the Great Depression, although to claim the latter economic disaster was the sole reason the Nazis came to power in 1933 would however be a grave mistake. The greatest significance of the Munich Putsch was that when disaster struck Germany in 1929 the Nazis hit the ground running. The party and its leader had already done the groundwork from 1925. It was ready to meet the needs of those who needed an alternative to democracy. Its leader was ready, thanks to Munich, to meet his self-prophesied destiny. The Nazis and Hitler needed Munich to find their role. The fact that they were political 'failures' between 1924–29 made no difference as their avenue to power was opened with the economic slump.

WEIMAR ECONOMY

Source 1

It pounds daily on the nerves: the insanity of numbers, the uncertain future, today, and tomorrow become doubtful once more overnight. An epidemic of fear, naked need: lines of shoppers … form in front of shops, first in front of one, then in front of all … The lines always send the same signal: the city, the big stone city will be shopped empty again. Rice, 80,000 marks a pound yesterday, costs 160,000 marks today, and tomorrow perhaps twice as much … The piece of paper, the spanking brand-new bank note, still moist from the printers, paid out today as a weekly wage, shrinks in value on the way to the grocer's shop. The zeros, the multiplying zeros!

Extract from the newspaper *Berliner Illustrirte Zeitung* (Illustrated News), 26 August 1923
The article by the historical observer Friedrich Kroner was entitled 'Overwrought Nerves'.

Source 2

… Germany's growing and industrious population; her great technical skill; the wealth of her material resources; the development of her agriculture on progressive lines; her eminence in industrial science; all these factors enable us to be hopeful with regard to her future production …

Germany is therefore well equipped with resources; she possesses the means for exploiting them on a large scale; when the present credit shortage has been overcome, she will be able to resume a favoured position in the activity of a world where normal conditions of exchange are gradually being restored.

Extract from The Dawes Committee Report, 1924
'Text of the Dawes Committee Report', *World Peace Foundation Pamphlets* 7, no 5 (1924)
This report led to the implementation of the Dawes Plan. The Dawes Plan brought about easier reparations instalments, and a large investment of money into Germany.

Source 3

It must be remembered, however, that this recovery owed a great deal to the large amount of foreign aid flowing into Germany between 1924 and 1929, attracted by the prospects for investment in a country whose economic development was also carefully watched over by Allied representatives carrying out the Dawes Plan …

Moreover, German governments were hardly able to ensure that the recovery benefited all sections of German society and thus to remove the dangerous political discontent …

… wealth [transferred] from the thrifty cautious sections of the lower middle class to the industrialists and financiers … high unemployment levels in the latter 1920s marred the 'prosperous' Germany …

Nor did the situation in agriculture give cause for satisfaction … it is not surprising that rural support was also important to Hitler's movement, and in general the economic pressures in Weimar Germany go far towards explaining the difficulties in forming coalitions as well as the growing appeal of extremist parties.

From JW Hiden, *The Weimar Republic* (Longman, 1974)
Hiden talks about the reality of the so-called economic 'recovery' of Weimar Germany from 1924–29.

Q1

Study Source 1. How useful is it as evidence for a historian studying the hyperinflation crisis in Weimar Germany in 1923?

Usefulness for the study of the Weimar economy	
Date/Context	Written in August 1923 at the height of the hyperinflation crisis, the document gives us a clear contemporary insight into the period from someone who saw the crisis first-hand, along with its devastating effects on various sections of the population.
Author	Written by the historical observer Kroner, the document should be accurate in content, giving us a reliable account.

Mode	Taken from the newspaper *Berliner Illustrirte Zeitung*, the extract is extremely useful as it allows us to read just what contemporaries read at the height of the crisis, enabling us to understand the crisis first-hand.
Target audience	As a newspaper article, it can be assumed that the target audience is the general public. It is likely that many individuals would have easily identified with this article entitled 'Overwrought Nerves', making it a useful tool for understanding the depth of public feeling during the crisis.
Tone/ Language	The opening sentence reflects the desperation of the entire article when it uses such words and phrases as "nerves", "insanity" and "uncertain future". Indeed, the title of the article sets the 'stress' tone from the outset. This emotive language is useful as it allows us as historians to understand and empathise with the common man during the economic crisis.
Content	The content is extremely useful for understanding the daily plight of the common man in Germany. Hopelessness, uncertainty and fear dominate the article, along with "need". The extract discusses the queues in front of shops combined with increasingly escalating food prices, and finishes with a discussion of "moist" money fresh "from the printers". All of the latter we know to be the unfortunate reality for many Germans during the hyperinflation crisis.
Motive/ Purpose	As a historical observer, it is likely Friedrich Kroner is simply doing his job and writing about life. Like most pundits, however, there may well be a clear political motive behind this article. There is no doubt that the extensive use of emotive language throughout this article is deliberate and goes beyond that of a 'writer's style'. This could suggest that the article has been written to put pressure on the government by highlighting the plight of the common man, or, on a more basic level, the article's emotion may simply be a tool to help sell papers.

Limitations	The extract deals with the hyperinflation crisis and its impact on Germany, but fails to mention: ◆ reasons how and why the crisis began, including such issues as the German failure to pay the second instalment of its reparations bill as set out under the terms of the Treaty of Versailles, as well as the subsequent invasion by French and Belgian forces of the Ruhr ◆ that some Germans, like the major industrialist Hugo Stinnes, actually benefited from the hyperinflation crisis, for example by paying off loans with devalued money or buying up businesses with reserves of foreign currency ◆ how the crisis was resolved with the printing of money being stopped, the ending of passive resistance, and the introduction of a new currency, the Rentenmark, under the new chancellor Gustav Stresemann

Q2

Sources 1 and 2 provide different contemporary accounts of the economic situation in Weimar Germany in the 1920s. *How* and *why* do they differ?

How		
Themes	**Source 1**	**Source 2**
Date/Context	26 August 1923	1924
Author	Friedrich Kroner	Dawes Committee
Mode	Newspaper extract	Report
Target audience	General public	US government/ potential investors
Tone/Language	Downbeat in tone, emphasis on insanity and uncertainty, fear and endless queues	Positive outlook throughout, summarised by words and phrases like "growing", "industrious population", "wealth", and "eminence"

Content	• Uncertain future with overnight changes • Fear and need • Line of shoppers queuing for food • Inflation – rice 80,000 yesterday, 160,000 today • Paper money still wet from printers • Shrinking wages	• Population industrious, great in technical skill • Progressive agriculture • Eminence in industrial science – hopeful for future production • Germany well equipped • Germany as able to resume a favoured position in the world

Why		
Themes	**Source 1**	**Source 2**
Context	**Basic difference overview** Written at the height of hyperinflation crisis **Context** • Germany had faced increasing inflation before 1914. The situation had obviously become worse by the end of 1918 with defeat in war. • The reparations bill was set at £6.6 billion in 1921, with the first instalment (£100 million) by 1922. • Germany only paid £50 million in 1922 and made no payment in January 1923, claiming they could not afford it.	**Basic difference overview** Written to provide grounds for investment in Germany by American investors and entrepreneurs **Context** • Germany's hyperinflation crisis was upsetting the economic balance of Europe. • Both Britain and France had defaulted on their war debts to the US, claiming that they could not afford to pay as the German reparation payments had not filtered through to them.

	• French and Belgian troops (no British) invaded the Ruhr Valley in an attempt to take what was owed. • The response of the Weimar government was to call for passive resistance for all workers. The government, with limited funds, still had to pay these workers. French officials discovered the Germans were printing money, foreign investment was removed and confidence dropped in the German mark. The result was beyond inflation levels previously seen – hyperinflation.	• Under the leadership of Gustav Stresemann, passive resistance was ended (much to the annoyance of right wing nationalists who saw this as surrender to the French), the printing of money was stopped, and a new currency, the Rentenmark, was established (based on land values, not gold). Hjalmar Schacht had been the chief exponent of the latter measures.
Motive/ Purpose	• Kroner was a historical observer and interested in writing about daily events. • Kroner would have been paid to write such articles by the newspaper, perhaps simply to identify with the public on a humanitarian level or to put pressure on the government to end the hardship of the common man. • Kroner's account may have been a plea for help seeking an international audience. • The terrible situation in Germany for the majority of people was reason enough to write a piece like this in such a descriptive way.	• The report is probably very 'glowing' to provide potential investors with ample reason to take a financial risk by investing in Europe. • The US government needed the Dawes Plan to work to stimulate not only the German market but also to give the British and French no excuse for non-repayment of loans.

Q3

Using the sources *and* your own knowledge, assess the success of the Weimar economy in the period 1924–29.

Background

The hyperinflation crisis took hold in Germany after the French invasion of the Ruhr in January 1923, and had devastating consequences (Source 1). After Stresemann's appointment as chancellor in August, he took the brave political decision to end passive resistance on 26 September and, with the financial genius of Hjalmar Schacht, introduced the new Rentenmark currency on 15 November. While the new currency was needed, its stability rested not on gold but on the mortgaging of German land and industry. This was not a satisfactory long-term solution but one that was made easier with international intervention. The Dawes Committee (named after the chairman of the panel of financial experts) had begun work in October 1923 to address the issue of reparations and develop a new plan. Money was raised (some 800 million gold marks) mainly in America, largely due to the glowing report of Germany's economic potential (Source 2) and a loan given to the stricken German people. Reparations were adjusted to a moderate level of £50 million per annum for the following 5 years, rising to £125 million per annum thereafter. Beginning on 1 September 1924, the Dawes Plan signalled the sound of recovery, but at what cost and what depth? Any discussion of these issues must remain within the clear understanding that any recovery made during 1924–29 was based primarily on the large input of foreign investment.

The table opposite provides a brief overview of the successes or failures of key areas within the Weimar economy.

Key areas	Success	Failure
Industry	• Some economic growth	• Growth unsteady • Failure to impact on world markets • Growth of cartels (economic groups of 'large concern') which squashed the small businessmen
Agriculture		• Little recovery after First World War • Small farmers suppressed by landlords and government, causing demoralisation
Trade deficit (export values lower than imports)		• In every year, except 1926, trade deficit was a problem, therefore the country was losing money.
Prices	• Steady in majority of economic areas	• Agricultural prices drop
Unemployment		• Always above 1,000,000
Social welfare	• Welfare schemes extended	• Increased costs
Government		• High taxes and continual budget deficit (government spending more than it receives)

Economic and political effects (Source 3)

Peasant farmers felt increasingly overlooked by the government and were therefore hostile to democracy – many looked to the Nazis after 1929. Large landowners and the Junkers grew to dislike the system of government and looked for an authoritarian alternative.

Employers (whilst having made a deal with the government in 1919 to improve the workers' conditions) became increasingly hostile at high welfare costs that reduced profits at a time of limited, if not non-existent growth. Workers, while benefiting from the welfare system, made only modest financial gains. Overall, the large body of wealth that did exist passed from the hands of the lower middle classes to industrialists and financiers.

The economy as a whole was utterly dependent on US loans – of some 25.5 billion marks that flowed into Germany from foreign investment, 22.9 billion marks were paid out for reparation.

Success?

While the period 1924–29 saw Weimar Germany 'brought in from the cold' both politically and economically, it was never a permanent arrangement. While the Wall Street crash could not have been predicted in itself, even Stresemann recognised Germany's precarious position at the "edge of a volcano". Germany's 'recovery' was ultimately borrowed.

POLITICAL CRISIS 1930–33

Source 1

... I was sitting around surrounded by thousands of SA men and as Hitler spoke I was most interested at the shouts and more often the muttered exclamations of the men around me, who were mainly workmen or lower-middle-class types. 'He speaks for me, he speaks for me.' 'Ach Gott [Oh God], he knows how I feel.' Many of them seemed lost to the world around them and were probably unaware of what they were saying.

**From Amy E Buller, *Darkness Over Germany*
(Longmans, Green & Co, 1943)
Buller was an English religious commentator who, after having visited Germany in the 1930s, became an anti-Nazi. The SA event described occurred in the early 1930s, before Hitler was appointed chancellor.**

Source 2

Schleicher came to Hindenburg therefore with a demand for emergency powers as a prerequisite of action against the Nazis ... [and] believed it to be necessary to dissolve ... the Reichstag ... on the basis of Article 48.

... Hindenburg at once evinced grave doubts as to its constitutionality ... [and] declared that he was unable to give him such a blank cheque ... [Schleicher] tendered his resignation on 28 January.

... [Hindenburg] was opposed to the Nazis up to the last moment ... At Papen's suggestion, a meeting had been arranged between Hitler and Oskar von Hindenburg ...

... the Nazis had to be taken into the Government.

**Extract from Otto Meissner's Nuremberg Tribunal account in 1945, regarding the political developments leading to Hitler's appointment as chancellor
Meissner was state secretary in the Reich president's office.
J Noakes and G Pridham (eds), *Nazism 1919–1945, vol 1*
(University of Exeter Press, 1998)**

Source 3

For all his electoral successes, there has never been any doubt that Hitler came into office as the result of a backstairs political intrigue. 'The Germans' did not elect Hitler Reich Chancellor ... some have argued that the Weimar Republic destroyed itself rather than being destroyed by its enemies: a case of political suicide rather than political murder ... But [Germany's] ills were not just of the Republic's own making. Crucial to the whole process was the way in which democracy's enemies exploited the democratic ... political culture for their own ends. Joseph Goebbels [said]:

The stupidity of democracy. It will always remain one of democracy's best jokes that it provided its deadly enemies with the means by which it was destroyed.

From Richard J Evans, *The Coming of the Third Reich* (Penguin Books, 2003)

Q1

Study Source 1. How useful is it as evidence for a historian studying the rise of Hitler to power in the period 1930–33?

Usefulness for the study of the political crisis	
Date/Context	Written in 1943, the source is useful in that it was written during the Nazi era. While after the events of 1930–33, it does give us a more reflective, and perhaps objective, viewpoint from which to study the rise of Hitler to the position of chancellor of Germany.
Author	Amy E Buller was, as stated, a religious commentator. As an anti-Nazi, Buller's account is extremely useful in that it paints a powerful picture of the impact of Hitler's speech on the masses and how they identified with it, rather than a bleak, distasteful report we might expect from an anti-Nazi individual.

Mode	Published in the book *Darkness over Germany*, the extract is useful in that it gives us the information that was being released to the general public regarding the rise of Hitler to power.
Target audience	It is difficult to know precisely which 'general public' this book was on sale to. While it is most certainly aimed at contemporaries of the Nazi period, there is little chance anyone in Germany would have found this work in a book store. The reality is that this publication was on sale in Britain or the USA.
Tone/ Language	As far as the extract goes, it appears to be written in a journalistic style. Filled with quotations from various SA men, Buller herself also comments on the situation with the phrase "lost to the world". This kind of language could be seen as 'sensationalist'. Indeed, the title of the work leaves the reader in no doubt as to the opinion of its author. While useful, this extract therefore needs to be treated with care.
Content	Writing from the position of listening to a speech, Buller's account shows us just how influential and intelligent Hitler's speech-making was. With statements from SA men claiming "He speaks for me" and "he knows how I feel", we can assume that the speech was touching on issues important to those listening. Interestingly, Buller goes one step further by suggesting that many of these men "seemed lost to the world around them", caught in a trance-like state. The source is therefore very useful in understanding the rise of Hitler to power, not only by giving us evidence of Hitler's personal role and skills, but also by showing us the power of Nazi propaganda and its ability to touch the hearts of those listening. We can also see from this account the power of mass rallies which were so important in the rise of Hitler and the Nazi Party to power.
Motive/ Purpose	When any book is published it is difficult not to mention money when considering a purpose for publication. Other motives may be that the author wants to let the 'free' world know just how influential and powerful Hitler is, but not in an adoring way; to explain the phenomenon that is National Socialism; or to elevate herself above the German masses as

	one able to see Hitler for who he really is. Whatever the reason, Buller's book would have made good reading to those during the Second World War searching for answers to Hitler's rise to power.
Limitations	While the source is useful for understanding the impact of mass rallies and Hitler's skill as a speech-writer and maker, the extract fails to mention: • the precise role of the SA, in both propaganda and violence towards other parties and their deputies (especially the Communists) • the aims and manifesto of the Nazi party and their appeal to the masses • the role of Joseph Goebbels and other forms of propaganda • the impact of the Great Depression and the obvious increase in Nazi votes as a result • the failure/weakness of democracy and Weimar's 'centre' political parties to establish clear principles and actions against the increasing rise of political extremism • the role of political intrigue, especially by General Kurt von Schleicher and Franz von Papen. • the role of Hindenburg and the elite

Q2

Sources 1 and 2 provide different contemporary reasons for Hitler's appointment as chancellor in 1933. *How* and *why* do they differ?

How		
Themes	**Source 1**	**Source 2**
Date/Context	1943	1945
Author	Amy E Buller	Otto Meissner
Mode	Book, *Darkness Over Germany*	Nuremberg Tribunal
Target audience	General public	Prosecution/Defence at trial
Tone/Language	Report, emotive quotations	Factual, reporting style
Content	• Thousands of SA men listening to Hitler • Caught up in emotion of event • Many lost to world around them and unaware of what is around them • Power obtained via Hitler's personal/political skill	• Schleicher demands emergency powers • Hindenburg has doubts and Schleicher tenders resignation • Hindenburg opposed to Nazis but persuaded by von Papen and Oskar Hindenburg • Nazis make the government • Power obtained via political intrigue

Why		
Themes	**Source 1**	**Source 2**
Context	**Basic difference overview** Hitler's rise to power was based on his political skill and propaganda. **Context** • The period 1929–33 was one of vast political growth for extremist parties, especially the Nazis. • The Great Depression of October 1929 had resulted in a huge political swing away from 'democratic' parties, especially as they were, in the eyes of the public, failing to meet the needs of the people. • The Nazis were seen as a young, vibrant movement that promised to meet the people's needs ("Work and Bread") while defending Germany from the Communists. • Hitler was a great orator and propagandist, and made countless speeches during the early 1930s, highlighted by the 'Hitler over Germany' campaigns of 1932, organised by Goebbels.	**Basic difference overview** Hitler's rise to power was a result of political intrigue rather than personal skill. **Context** • 1930–32 saw a catalogue of changes in the chancellorship of Germany. It must be remembered that during this period no single chancellor, apart from Hitler, enjoyed a party with a majority within the Reichstag. • Muller and Bruning had been removed from office by President Hindenburg, after failing to solve the economic crisis created by the Great Depression. In each dismissal, Schleicher had helped the aging president in his decision. It was also under Schleicher's council that Hindenburg appointed his aristocratic friend, von Papen. Von Papen did not survive a vote of no confidence in mid-1932. Against the growing tide of Nazism, he stepped down from office, 'helped' by Schleicher who had

			been against von Papen's proposal to use emergency powers (Article 48). • Having in effect made himself chancellor, Schleicher was also removed from office after he too asked for emergency powers. Hindenburg had little choice but to appoint Hitler (although after persuasion from von Papen and his son Oskar).
Motive/Purpose		• It would have been easier to read a source from an anti-Nazi, such as Buller, which criticised Hitler. • The source attempts to show Hitler's audience, rather than Hitler himself, in a bad light. • Perhaps Buller wanted to show the oratorical skill of Hitler, illustrating his power and how the audience could be taken over – perhaps deflecting guilt from German people. • Buller may have wanted to show the control Hitler had over the SA. • Buller's title, *Darkness Over Germany*, may suggest a religious theme, with 'evil' consuming those SA men who are "unaware of what they were saying".	• It is doubtful Meissner would have lied to the Nuremberg Tribunal concerning the political intrigue behind Hitler's appointment. • He may have wished to blame Hindenburg, or more likely Schleicher, for Hitler's rise to power, but this is difficult to tell from the style of the account. • Meissner's motives may have been to play down the power of Nazi propaganda and the role of Hitler in the run-up to his rise to power.

Q3

Using the sources *and* your own knowledge, assess the significance of political intrigue in the Nazis' rise to power in January 1933.

Factors in Hitler's rise to power

Long term:

+ Authoritarian/Militarism traditions
+ The legacy of the First World War
+ The limited German Revolution
+ The Weimar Constitution
+ The Treaty of Versailles
+ The hyperinflation crisis
+ The Munich Putsch
+ The unchecked growth of the Nazi Party between 1924–28

Short term:

+ Wall Street crash

+ Huge growth in unemployment

+ Electoral success of the Nazi Party in both presidential and Reichstag elections through the skill of Hitler (Source 1) and propaganda by Goebbels

+ The SA, both in propaganda and violence towards other political parties (especially the Communists)

+ The weakness of other successive chancellors to deal with the growing crisis, combined with their inability to see the danger of extremist parties, especially the Nazis

+ Political infighting and intrigue (Sources 2 and 3), especially by Schleicher and von Papen

+ The role of the elite and President Hindenburg

The perfect solution?

With all of the above factors responsible in some way or another for the rise of Hitler to power, it would be easy to forget the plight of the ordinary German citizen during this terrible crisis of 1929–33. Democracy had failed, but what remained? Choice was not something that most Germans, including the elite, felt they had. It cannot even be said that the people had two choices, either National Socialism or Communism, for together their votes added up to just over 50% of the total cast. Many Germans obviously voted along traditional lines as it was all they knew.

Realities

The truth is that the German people had no choice. While Hitler's Nazi Party became the largest party in the Reichstag by 1932, thereby gaining the 'moral' right to the chancellorship, Hitler was continually blocked by the aging Hindenburg (and Schleicher). Hindenburg held all the keys to power and, since the 1930s, he had used his presidential decrees to appoint chancellors without them having the majority vote or support of the Reichstag. By the end of 1932, Hitler was as far away from the job of chancellor as he was in the dark days of the 1920s. Indeed, some historians would suggest that the Nazi Party was as good as finished after the elections of November 1932, as its share of the electorate declined by some two million.

The goal

Hitler achieved power as a result of all of the above long- and short-term factors. His party was, without question, rescued by von Papen and Oskar von Hindenburg who persuaded the president to appoint Hitler to the position of chancellor. Without this approval, Hitler would never have achieved his goal. The people of Germany did not decide on his accession to power, nor, electorally, did he have the consent of the majority – Hindenburg was the controller. What we must not forget, however, is that Hitler had driven the Nazi Party and himself into the prime seat of German politics and into becoming 'leaders' of the Reichstag. The Nazis were the top political party as a result of many things, but not of political intrigue. The Nazis had earned the right to take the top job and perhaps it could be said that Hindenburg, the only person in Germany with a choice, had no real choice at all.

NAZI CONSOLIDATION OF POWER 1933–34

Source 1

… lorries with SA and SS had driven up at 4.05 p.m. The porter promptly closed the doors. But the Nazis broke the big display windows and pushed into the building through the holes. They opened fire inside the building with a number of rifles and revolvers. During this, the 28-year-old salesman, Hans Saile, the advertising manager of the Advertising Union, Berlin, was killed by a shot in the stomach …

The intruders rushed up the stairs and smashed in the locked doors with their rifle butts. Union secretaries, employees, typists, Co-op salesgirls were all driven together with cudgels, rifles, revolvers and daggers … The whole building was searched for valuables. Then the swastika flag was hoisted …

The regular police had meanwhile blocked off the surrounding streets with a strong force. The Nazis looted the building in front of their very eyes.

Extract from a SOPADE (Social Democratic Party in exile) report in 1933 to the Executive Committee in Prague
The report focuses on the role of the SA in consolidating power for the Nazi Party in the state of Brunswick.
J Noakes and G Pridham (eds), *Nazism 1919–1945, vol 1* (University of Exeter Press, 1998)

Source 2

By the authority of Section 48 (2) of the German Constitution the following is decreed as a defensive measure against Communist acts of violence endangering the State:

… restrictions on personal liberty, on the right of free expression of opinion, including freedom of the press, on the right of assembly and association, and violations of the privacy of postal, telegraphic and telephonic communications, and warrants for house-searches, orders for confiscations as well as restrictions on property rights are permissible beyond the legal limits otherwise prescribed.

Extract from the Decree of the Reich President for the Protection of the People and State, 28 February 1933
This was issued one day after the Reichstag fire.
J Noakes and G Pridham (eds), *Nazism 1919–1945, vol 1* (University of Exeter Press, 1998)

Source 3

... 89.9 per cent of the voters supported Hitler's constitutionally now unlimited powers as head of state, head of government, leader of the party, and Supreme Commander of the armed forces. The result ... reflected the fact that Hitler had the backing, much of it fervently [ie passionately] enthusiastic, of the great majority of the German people.

... He was now institutionally unchallengeable ... adored by much of the population. He had secured total power. The Führer state was established. Germany had bound itself to the dictatorship it had created.

**From Ian Kershaw, *Hitler: 1889–1936: Hubris*
(Allen Lane, The Penguin Press, 1998)
After the death of President Hindenburg on 2 August 1934, Hitler merged the offices of chancellor and president. To ensure public support for this decision, Hitler held a plebiscite – a vote by the whole electorate.**

Q1

Study Source 1. How useful is it as evidence for a historian studying Nazi consolidation of power?

Usefulness for the study of the Nazi consolidation of power	
Date/Context	Written in 1933, this document is very useful for a historian studying Nazi consolidation of power between 1933–34. Written at the outset of the period, this contemporary document gives us the opportunity to learn of the process from people at that time.
Author	Written by an 'agent' or insider for the SOPADE, or Social Democratic Party in exile, this source is extremely useful in that it gives us a non-Nazi explanation for the consolidation process. It may therefore be less likely to be prejudiced as these reports were designed to be largely informative on the nature of events in Germany.

Mode	As a report that focuses on the role of the SA in consolidating power, this source is very useful in terms of the question as it clearly shows how the Storm Troopers operated at a local level and their relevant power within individual Lander (states).
Target audience	Written for the Executive Committee of the SOPADE who were in exile in Prague at this time, the report is of importance as it was not meant for public consumption. It should therefore avoid the possible sensationalism of a newspaper report.
Tone/ Language	Devoid of emotion, the source's style is simply informative, reading like a simple series of events with no comment from its author. This makes it very useful as it removes bias from the information and allows us untainted access to the role of the SA in the Nazi consolidation of power.
Content	The source gives us very precise details of an SA and SS raid on a building. Having forced their way in and killed en route, the SA and SS proceed to search "for valuables" and then raise the "swastika flag". The power of the SA and SS is undeniable in this account, as is their complete disregard for human life and decency. While the actions of the SA and SS are useful for this topic, perhaps what is more interesting is the role of the regular police who stand back and watch the Nazis loot "the building in front of their very eyes". From this we can surmise one of two things: either the SA and SS have the blessing of the regular police or the latter are powerless to stop them. Whatever the case, we as historians can clearly appreciate the violent role played by the Storm Troopers in Hitler's rise to power.
Motive/ Purpose	As a factual report to the Executive Committee of the SOPADE, the motive is quite simply to keep the SOPADE informed of events within Germany. The lack of emotion and comment from the author backs this up and adds weight to the argument that this is simply an information gathering exercise. This makes it extremely useful in understanding the methods used by the Nazis in consolidating power.

Limitations	While useful, there are many limitations to this source regarding the question. There are two, almost distinct, sides to the Nazi consolidation of power process, in terms of legal and violent methods. While this source deals with an aggressive incident, it fails to mention major events which were vital to the consolidation process, such as: • the Reichstag fire and subsequent Law for the Protection of the People and State • the Enabling Act • the banning of Trade Unions • the Law Against the Formation of New Parties • the concordat with the Roman Catholic Church • the Night of the Long Knives • the death of Hindenburg • the oath of allegiance sworn to Hitler by the army While the list is far from complete, most of the above events can be used, as in the case of the Enabling Act, as evidence for both legal and violent methods used by the Nazis to consolidate their power between 1933–34.

Q2

Sources 1 and 2 provide different contemporary methods of Nazi consolidation of power in Germany. How and why do they differ?

How		
Themes	Source 1	Source 2
Date/Context	1933	28 February 1933
Author	SOPADE agent in Germany	Reich president Paul von Hindenburg – although supplied by Nazi Party officials
Mode	Report	Decree

55

Target audience	Executive Committee of the SOPADE	The German people
Tone/Language	Informative yet devoid of emotion	Authoritative and commanding
Content	• Lorries with SA and SS break into building • Salesman shot dead • Threatening behaviour towards all individuals and building looted • Strong police force stand by and allow terror to occur	• Defensive action against Communism • Removal of personal liberties including freedom of speech, freedom of press, and right of assembly • Above measures undertaken via authority of German Constitution

Why		
Themes	Source 1	Source 2
Context	**Basic difference overview** Use of terror and violence to consolidate chancellorship **Context** • While the Nazis had decided in 1924 to become a political movement and seize power legally, violence was never far from the heart of the party. The 1930–33 period saw an ever-increasing role for the SA (Storm Troopers) and many of the growing numbers of the unemployed sought refuge and status within its ranks.	**Basic difference overview** Use of constitutional, legal methods to consolidate chancellorship **Context** • On gaining the chancellorship, Hitler was far from being politically secure and immediately sought permission from Hindenburg to dissolve the Reichstag and call new elections on 5 March. Hitler wanted the necessary 50% majority.

	• With over 2 million in its ranks by 1933 and led by the ultra-violent Ernst Röhm, the SA became a law into itself and felt nothing towards the general public who grew steadily to dislike its mob-like behaviour. • The SA was superior in numbers to the army (although secretly numbered as part of the Reichswehr since its foundation in the early 1920s), and Röhm began to call out for a 'Second Revolution', the development of a truly National Socialist state. • The SA in effect had no equal and had many supporters in the elite who saw them as the defenders of Germany against Communism – this 'support' quickly faded as violence escalated.	• On 27 February, one week before the elections, the Reichstag went up in flames – ex-Communist Marianus van der Lubbe was found at the scene and accused. • On 28 February, the Decree of the Reich President for the Protection of the Nation and State was issued.
Motive/ Purpose	• Reports such as these were simply to provide a realistic image of life in Nazi Germany, outside of propaganda. The motive of this source is to give a clear example of the methodology and police 'support' to the members of the SOPADE.	• While the president issued the decree, the document had been prepared by the Nazis some time before. However, this is not to suggest that the Nazis had planned and executed the Reichstag fire, which historians like Kershaw believe to be the independent action of van der Lubbe.

	• Its factual nature is reflected by the lack of emotion throughout.	• This law was primarily intended for use against the KPD, allowing the Nazis to arrest and hold indefinitely any deputy or activist. This was a useful weapon against the Communists, who were certainly a threat in the run-up to the elections.
		• While the decree was originally intended to be temporary, this law had the potential to be, and did eventually become, the virtual law of the Third Reich, suspending constitutional civil rights of every individual within Germany. It is hard to imagine Hitler and Goering (a chief aide in the drafting of the decree) not having envisaged such a law being extended.

Q3

Using the sources *and* your own knowledge, assess to what extent Hitler's consolidation of power was legal in the period 1933–34.

This question is in some ways clear-cut in that Hitler came to power with only two other members of his cabinet being Nazis. From this position of weakness, and under the careful eye of von Papen, Hitler outmanoeuvred his opponents with such pace that by August of the following year he had merged the offices of chancellor and president and was, in reality, constitutionally untouchable. This could not have been achieved solely by using violence. President Hindenburg, until his death in August 1934, retained the power to remove Hitler at any time, but did not. Hitler's path to power was one of great skill, supreme opportunity and of course, as before his appointment, a lack of united opposition.

Hitler's methods in consolidating power

Date	Methods	Legal/ Terror	Explanation/Consequence
27 February 1933	Reichstag fire	Terror (although not Nazi-initiated)	This is believed now to be the sole work of Marianus van der Lubbe (though the debate rages on). Hitler and Goering were able to persuade Hindenburg to pass the Decree of the Reich President for the Protection of the People and State.
28 February 1933	The Decree of the Reich President for the Protection of the People and State	Legal	This law was brought into effect to prevent a Communist revolution. Communist deputies and sympathisers were rounded up and sent to Dachau. A week of arrests and violence was nicknamed 'The Brown Terror' as the SA smashed their political opponents. The KPD were banned from the forthcoming elections. The Decree became a virtual law of the Third Reich as it was never repealed.
5 March 1933	Elections	Legal	With the KPD gone, Hitler should have been able to gain the necessary 50% majority. He got only 44%, even with the highest voter turnout of 88.8%. While disappointed, Hitler merged with the much smaller Nationalist Party, taking their 8% and thereby achieving his majority in the Reichstag.
13 March 1933	New Ministry for Public Enlightenment and Propaganda	Legal	Hitler was now able to move state money into Nazi propaganda and begin to control the flow of information in and around Germany, as well as censoring outside material.

24 March 1933	Enabling Act	Legal/ Terror	While Hitler did gain the necessary 66% of the vote to make this constitutional change, by a vote of 441 to 94, the SA and SS had surrounded the Kroll Opera House before the deputies had arrived. No doubt intimidation played a role with some deputies. The Act allowed Hitler to make laws for four years without the consent of the president or Reichstag. Hitler (and his cabinet) were given the right to pass emergency laws. This law became the new constitution of the Third Reich.
14 July 1933	Law Against the Formation of New Parties	Legal	While legal, this law backed up previous months of terror and intimidation of other political parties by the SA. By the time this law had been passed, only the Nazi Party remained. Germany became a one-party state.
January 1934	Law for the Reconstruction of the State	Legal/ Terror	While all elected state assemblies were dissolved and new 'Reich Governors' replaced them, this process had begun many months before with SA intimidation, violence and murders. The law passed in January formalised what had already come to pass.

30 June 1934	Night of the Long Knives	Terror	With the death toll ranging between 70 and 1,000, we can be sure that Röhm and most of the leadership of the SA were executed by the SS. While Hitler also used the opportunity to remove 'old enemies' like Schleicher, this event helped Hitler's reputation with the general public and the German army. Hitler was now seen as a defender of the German people from those who would seek to destroy Germany.
1–2 August 1934	Law Concerning the Head of State of the German Reich Death of Hindenburg	Legal	With the merging of offices, Hitler became Führer and Reich president on 1 August. After Hindenburg's death on 2 August, the army swore an oath of personal loyalty to Hitler.

While the above events cover but a few of the many methods used by Hitler and the Nazi Party to consolidate power, they do show that, on the surface at least, Hitler used mainly legal means to consolidate and execute his power. This 'legal' perception was important to uphold in the mind of the German public and the outside world, and it was one that was ruthlessly and brilliantly upheld and developed by Goebbels and his propaganda machine.

Few would have guessed that Hitler, in such a short space of time, would have gained so much. His opponents were simply unable to grasp just how effective the Nazis could be. In fact, some, like von Papen in the gaining of the concordat agreement between the Vatican and state, were prepared to help the Nazis on their way.

Nazi economy

Source 1

What we have achieved in two and a half years in the way of a planned provision of labour, a planned regulation of the market, a planned control of prices and wages, was considered a few years ago to be absolutely impossible. We only succeeded because ... we had the living energies of the whole nation. We had, however, first to create a number of technical and psychological conditions before we could carry out this purpose ... first of all to put a stop to the everlasting fluctuations of wages and prices. It was further necessary to remove the conditions giving rise to interference ... i.e. to destroy the class organisations [ie Trade Unions] of both ... employers and employees ... Here arose the necessity for a new conservative and vital constitution and a new organisation of the Reich and state.

Extract from a speech by Hitler to the Reichstag, 21 May 1935, explaining his economic success

Source 2

The small businessmen are in a state of gloom and despondency [ie hopelessness]. These people, to whom the present system to a large extent owes its rise, are the most disappointed of all. The shortages of goods restrict their turnover ... The artisans complain about raw material shortages ... one can say of many of them (the small businessmen) that inwardly they have long since turned away from the system and would welcome its fall.

Extract from a report written in 1939 for the SOPADE in Paris, on the economic situation in central Germany
The report clearly shows complaints about the Nazi economic policy.

Source 3

Hitler had no special recipe for the German economy when he came to power. There was no package of Nazi policies developed and ready to bring about revival ... Rearmament dominated Germany's economy between 1936 and 1939; it is difficult to argue in this period that Germany was programmed for anything except the very largest preparation for war ...

[But] When war broke out in 1939 it was not the war that Hitler had expected ... the problem Germany faced in 1941 was a relatively modest level of weapons output ... When it was discovered that Germany hardly had any more tanks and aircraft to attack Russia than she had had to attack Poland two years before, Hitler was astonished.

From Richard Overy (Professor of Modern History at King's College, London), 'The Nazi Economy: Success or Failure' (*Modern History Review*, vol 7, no 4, April 1996)

Q1

Study Source 1. How useful is it as evidence for a historian studying Nazi economic successes in the period 1933–36?

Usefulness for the study of the Nazi economy	
Date/Context	Given on 21 May 1935, this speech is of great use for a historian studying economic successes of the Nazis between 1933–39. A contemporary document, this source gives us a first-hand insight into the Nazi economy.
Author	The speech was given by Hitler. If anyone could trumpet the success of Nazi economic policies, it would be him. As leader of the party, it is useful to see what Hitler himself claims to be a success, and therefore this source is of great importance.
Mode	While we need to be careful with any speech given by Hitler due to its propaganda value, the format still allows us to see what information was being relayed on a 'public' level. This makes the source very useful for studying economic successes, as it highlights what Hitler felt was important to mention and, perhaps more importantly, what he left out.

Target audience	While this speech was given to the Reichstag, two things need to be remembered. Firstly, since July 1933 and the Law Against the Formation of New Parties, the Reichstag had contained only Nazi deputies. Secondly, all speeches given by Hitler to the Reichstag were conveyed to the public via the national press. Therefore, this speech is not only for the ears of the party but also the population of Germany.
Tone/ Language	The tone of this extract begins in a triumphant manner, using such words as "achieved" and "succeeded" in reference to Nazi economic policies. Hitler leaves us in no doubt that he is proud of what he has achieved, but in the second half of the extract he suggests it has not been plain sailing, saying "We had, however, first to create …" While Hitler could be apologising for the actions of price fixing, the removal of Trade Unions, and the creation of a new constitution, this would not fit with his current status as Führer and Reich chancellor at that time.
Content	According to Hitler, the Nazis have achieved an economic miracle in just two and a half years, with planned labour, regulation of the market, and control of prices and wages. When looking back on the government of Weimar, Hitler's statement, that these changes would have been "considered a few years ago to be absolutely impossible", was entirely accurate.
	His speech follows these successes with claims that certain measures had to be taken in order to make these changes – namely to remove the "everlasting fluctuations" of prices and wages, remove the Trade Unions of both employers and employees, as well as creating a new constitution for, and new organisation of, the Reich.
	This source is of great importance in the study of Nazi economic successes in that Hitler, the leader of Germany, clearly identifies what he believes to be the defining measures.
	Also, while this speech has obvious propaganda value, he does touch on what is accurate and truthful regarding what has been achieved by 1935 (even though his reasons for the destruction of Trade Unions and creation of a new constitution remain subjective to say the least).

Motive/ Purpose	While the source is of great use for any historian studying the economic successes of the Nazis, it is doubtful that this speech was designed to celebrate success simply for its own sake. The bulk of this extract is an unmistakable justification for the imposition of new rules and regulations in Germany. While many measures were "necessary" for Hitler to consolidate his position, few would call his constitution "conservative" and, combined with a restructuring of the state, no one had a choice. This speech was not needed to convince the Reichstag, or indeed the public, of Hitler's prowess in the economy. Rather, it would seem that Hitler simply needed the backdrop of the economy to justify his changes.
Limitations	While the source has many uses, it also has its limitations in understanding all of the economic success in the period 1933–36. For example, it: ✦ deals with the period up to 1935, and not 1936 ✦ makes no mention of Hjlamar Schacht and the Four Year Plan ✦ fails to develop the ongoing issue of the balance of trade deficit ✦ neglects to mention the secret rearmament programme which helped to stimulate the economy, as well as the accompanying MEFO bills which were used in part to pay for this ✦ mentions nothing of the increasing 'burnout' of the economy by 1936 and the so-called 'Guns or Butter' debate ✦ gives no hint of Hitler's growing desire to increase military spending by 1936, and Schacht's 'replacement' by Herman Goering under a new economic department called the Office of the Four Year Plan

Q2

Sources 1 and 2 provide different contemporary accounts of Nazi economic success. *How* and *why* do they differ?

How		
Themes	**Source 1**	**Source 2**
Date/Context	21 May 1935	1939
Author	Hitler	Agent for SOPADE
Mode	Speech	Report
Target audience	Reichstag and German public	SOPADE Executive Committee
Tone/Language	Success and achievement	Depression and gloom, hopelessness, disappointment
Content	• Achieved planned labour, regulation of the market, and control of prices and wages • Changes made to allow change to happen • Removal of Trade Unions for both employees and employers • Introduction of new constitution and reorganisation of the state	• Small businessmen in state of gloom and hopelessness • Disappointment • Turnover restricted by shortage of goods • Raw material shortages • Many turning away from Nazis and would welcome the fall of the party

Why		
Themes	**Source 1**	**Source 2**
Context	**Basic difference overview** The Nazis have been extremely successful and have secured an economic miracle for the whole nation using regulations and restrictions. **Context** Schacht's economic miracle from public works to the New Plan had dramatically changed the prospects for Germany's future.	**Basic difference overview** Small businessmen are in a state of gloom and hopelessness. Shortages have left them questioning their loyalty to the Nazis and desiring their fall. **Context** With Schacht's 'removal', Goering's Office of the Four Year Plan had been rearming Germany at a rapid rate. Shortages of labour and raw materials were becoming apparent.
Motive/ Purpose	• Hitler's speech may have been to rally support among the people as it would have been printed in the newspapers, thereby enhancing his own personal power and developing the myth of the Führer. • The speech may have been more to do with Hitler's changes to the constitution than the economy. His discussion of the economy may have been a good propaganda tool to justify the Nazis' stricter control on domestic life. • Hitler may have wished to claim personal credit for Schacht's work.	• This report would have been commissioned by the Executive Committee on this particular topic. • The SOPADE agent had no reason to lie. Information gathered needed to be accurate to allow the Executive Committee of the SOPADE to gauge the growth and failures of the Nazis. • With no apparent exaggeration or bias, this source was simply a factual report.

Q3

Using the sources *and* your own knowledge, assess how successful Nazi economic policies were in the period 1933–39.

Background

The impact of the Depression had left its mark not only on Germany but also on its new leader. Hitler was acutely aware that the Wall Street crash had been a major contributing factor in his rise to power. He was also aware of the massive task that lay before him as he embraced the chancellorship – all chancellors from 1930 had failed to deal with the problem of the economy to the satisfaction of the people. To stay in power, Hitler needed results and he needed them instantly.

Uninterested in economics, Hitler turned to the awesome skills of Hjalmar Schacht (appointed as first president of the Reichsbank in March 1933) in much the same fashion as his chancellor predecessor Gustav Stresemann had done in 1923.

Hitler's aims vary over the 1933–39 period. Interestingly, the Nazis had no economic policies before coming to power (Source 3) even though throughout 1930–32 they had promised the people "Work and Bread".

Aims 1933–36 – RECOVERY

* Tackle the Depression – it had destroyed the previous regime.

* Restore full employment to Germany's workforce (six or possibly eight million were unemployed).

* On the basis of the above, Hitler would win the support of the people and consolidate his and his party's position.

* Begin to rebuild Germany's military might as a prelude to expansion. This final aim was largely kept secret from the general public.

* Develop a defence economy or Wehrwirtschaft, where materials needed for war are developed 'in-house' – Germany was short in raw materials and exports were low due to a slump in world trade.

Policies/Methods

+ Government increase of public expenditure and investment
+ Stimulation of consumer demand
+ Public Works schemes (initiated by von Papen in 1932)
+ Tax concessions to new industries and families
+ Destruction of independent unions
+ Conscription
+ Use of deficit financing
+ MEFO bills
+ Government controls on prices and wages via New Plan of 1934 (Sources 2 and 3)

Results

While there were those who had reason to grumble (Source 2), the above policies had a dramatic effect on unemployment, so much so that by 1936 there were only 1.6 million people without work. Confidence was restored to the greater part of the German people, and Hitler trumpeted his success (Source 1).

Caution?

+ The issue of reparations which had dogged Weimar had been taken care of at the Lausanne Conference of 1932, when they had been suspended. Hitler merely announced he was permanently stopping reparations and took the credit for von Papen's work.

+ Hitler's economic climate had also changed due to the natural upturn of the world economy since 1932.

+ Hitler's political environment allowed him to make tough decisions and introduce radical economic policies – Weimar politicians did not have this luxury.

Aims 1936–39 – REARMAMENT

+ Rearmament
+ Territorial expansion

Policies/Methods

+ Introduction of the Four Year Plan:

    + German economy to be fit for war in four years

    + Autarky fulfilled in four years, via domestic industrial expansion, development of substitute products, and territorial expansion

    + Extension of government controls

    + Rearmament on a vast scale

Results

The biggest result of these aims and methods was the development of the economy for ideological aspirations and desires. The 'removal' of Schacht and the introduction of Goering and his Office of the Four Year Plan would have dire consequences for the economy and Hitler's proposed lebensraum. By 1939 the economy was in danger of overheating, as there were major labour and raw material shortages, combined with an increase in some consumer goods prices. While this was a disaster for the decision to wage war (Source 3), interestingly the 'burnout' and rearmament programme did not lead to mass protests or opposition from the public, and neither did they cause a serious price inflation. The economy did not deliver in this period, but propaganda and terror did.

THE SS

Source 1

I know how mendaciously [ie untruthfully] and foolishly people abroad write and tell tales about and run down this institution. Concentration camp is certainly, like any form of deprivation of liberty, a tough and strict measure. Hard, productive labour, a regular life, exceptional cleanliness in matters of daily life and personal hygiene, splendid food, strict but fair treatment, instruction in learning how to work again and how to learn the necessary crafts – these are the methods of education. The motto which stands above these camps reads: there is a path to freedom. Its milestones are: obedience, hard work, honesty, orderliness, cleanliness, sobriety, truthfulness, self-sacrifice and love of the Fatherland.

Extract from a radio broadcast to the German public by Himmler, 21 September 1939, commenting on concentration camps
J Noakes and G Pridham (eds), *Nazism 1919–1945, vol 2* (University of Exeter Press, 2000)

Source 2

It is midday when a long line of women, children and old people enter the yard of the crematorium, people from the Lódź ghetto. One can see that they are exhausted and anxious. The senior official in charge ... tell[s] them that they are going to have a bath and that afterwards they will get a drink of hot coffee. There is applause ... They all undress in the yard. The doors of the crematorium open and they enter ... they realise they have fallen into a trap ... The first people to enter the gas chamber begin to draw back. They sense the death which awaits them ... For two endless minutes one can hear banging on the walls and screams which are no longer human. And then – not a sound.

Extract from an account written shortly after the war by Sigismund Bendel, a French doctor who was attached for a while to the Jewish 'special commando' (Jews forced to work by the SS within the concentration camps) in Birkenau
J Noakes and G Pridham (eds), *Nazism 1919–1945, vol 3* (University of Exeter Press, 2001)

Source 3

The Gestapo itself fostered its image as an all-powerful body that brought dread to the enemies of the regime. Such a belief in itself helped the Gestapo to intimidate the population. This view was also propounded (put forward) after the war by many Germans, who could thus excuse their passivity and broad acceptance of the regime by their fear of the all-powerful Gestapo.

However, some historians now argue that this image of the Gestapo is a myth … [and suggest] The might of the Gestapo was in fact much weaker and its power rested on popular consent more than on terror.

From John Hite and Chris Hinton, *Weimar and Nazi Germany* (Hodder Murray, 2000)

Q1

> *Study Source 1.* **How useful is it as evidence for a historian studying the role of concentration camps in Nazi Germany?**

Usefulness for the study of concentration camps	
Date/Context	Broadcast in 1939, just days after the outbreak of the Second World War and six years after the Nazis came to power, this contemporary document is very useful for any historian studying the role of concentration camps. It provides us with first-hand evidence from a leading Nazi as to their function.
Author	As head of the SS, there could be no better source for understanding the role of the concentration camp, albeit from a Nazi point of view. As was normal in the Third Reich, many leading Nazis interpreted laws/orders to varying degrees and this was certainly the case in SS-run camps. While some SS camp leaders may have had their own point of view on what the purpose of any camp was, this source, from the head of the SS, should leave us in no doubt as to their function, at least in the eyes of the German public.

Mode	As a radio broadcast, the extract is very useful to a historian. Through this medium we can see exactly the image Himmler wants to paint to the German public of the role of camps, just days after the outbreak of war.
Target audience	With the German public being the target, it is interesting that this broadcast was being made in the first place, as Germany had just gone to war. This makes the source very useful as Himmler must have felt it necessary to discuss this issue with the people, making the motive behind the broadcast even more intriguing.
Tone/ Language	This source is largely informative in nature but remains colourless in tone. There are clear statements about the functioning of camps and their harshness, but such information is not enhanced with threats or statements that declare their inhabitants are deserving, or awaiting, a fatal end. Again, this is likely to be a reflection of the mode of the source and the underlying motive behind its creation.
Content	The source appears to be a rebuttal against 'untruthful' comments made by those abroad about the system of concentration camps. While Himmler declares that the camps are "tough and strict", he follows this with claims that the camps are merely places where inmates can learn "how to work again" and that ultimately "there is a path to freedom". This of course goes against what we know of concentration camps and their incredible cruelty, making Himmler's use of the word "truthfulness" ironic.
Motive/ Purpose	The source can only be a counter-propaganda move to dispel rumours of the horrors of the camp system. During the war, censorship became an increasingly difficult task for Goebbels and the Propaganda Ministry and it is obvious from this source that cracks were appearing. This radio broadcast, designed to reach out to all Germans, is an attempt to steer the thoughts of those listening away from such rumours. While Himmler mentions hardships, he follows this with "splendid food, strict but fair treatment". This source is therefore very useful in understanding the role of camps in Germany, but only from the point of view of what the German public were told to believe.

Limitations	While important, this source leaves us with only a propaganda image of the purpose of camps. To understand fully the role of concentration camps in Nazi Germany we would need to: • look at writings or speeches of Himmler to SS camp leaders, where the treatment of prisoners is not as described in the extract • understand the type of prisoner in the camps, be they Jewish or otherwise • understand the progress of concentration camps into death camps outside Germany and the reasons for this, leading to the Final Solution • understand that concentration camps were part of life in Nazi Germany from 1933, and accepted as a necessary evil by the majority of the public

Q2

Sources 1 and 2 provide different contemporary accounts of the purpose of SS concentration camps. *How* and *why* do they differ?

How		
Themes	**Source 1**	**Source 2**
Date/Context	21 September 1939	Shortly after the war
Author	Himmler	Sigismund Bendel
Mode	Radio broadcast	Account
Target audience	General public in Germany	General public after the war
Tone/Language	Informative, although limited with the truth	Descriptive and emotive throughout
Content	• Camps are not as bad as described abroad. • They are a tough and strict measure.	• Camps are connected to crematoria and supplied by ghettoes.

• Treatment is strict but fair. • Camps are places of education, eg on cleanliness. • There is a path to freedom. • Truthfulness and self-sacrifice are milestones.	• Senior officials lie and offer baths to people, and they are told to undress. • They are taken to the crematorium and death is sensed. • There is no escape and they are gassed to death. The screams become inhuman.

Why		
Themes	**Source 1**	**Source 2**
Context	**Basic difference overview** Concentration camps are places of strict but fair measures. Their purpose is to educate their inmates in the love of the fatherland. **Context** • The SS were formed in 1925 as part of the SA. • Himmler became head in 1929 and head of the Bavarian police by 1933 (by 1936 all police forces were unified under his command). • The broadcast took place after the Night of the Long Knives in June 1934.	**Basic difference overview** Concentration camps are places of deception and extermination. **Context** • Persecution of the Jews had been a slow and gradual process since 1933. • The 1935 Nuremberg Law defined what a Jew was and removed their citizenship, paving the way for further legal actions.

	• By 1939 Himmler and the SS were charged with the task of strengthening German nationhood and were in full control of concentration camps. • Under Heydrich, the Final Solution was devised and implemented in specially transformed concentration camps.	• November 1938 and the Night of the Broken Glass saw the fate of the Jews being delivered into the hands of the SS and the infamous SD department headed by Reinhard Heydrich. • 1939 saw the advent of ghettoes and the beginning of slave labour en masse. These ghettoes were in effect concentration camps. • Only in 1939 were there calls by some of the Nazi hierarchy (eg Hans Frank, later Gauleiter of Poland) for a more permanent solution to the 'Jewish Question'. • At the Wannsee Conference in 1942, the Final Solution became 'policy' and concentration camps were adapted.
Motive/Purpose	• The broadcast was produced in 1939 as a direct result of outside allegations of 'inappropriate' measures being employed in concentration camps. The allies had sought to use a hard-hitting propaganda campaign against the Nazis at the beginning of the war.	• Bendel's account matches those of countless survivors of the holocaust. There can be little doubt that the account is authentic.

+ The broadcast also served to reinforce Nazi ideology to the German public: "obedience", "self-sacrifice", "love of the Fatherland". + It could be suggested that the broadcast was a subtle threat to the German people to stay loyal to the regime or face punishment.	+ Bendel's job of 'Sonderkommando' was horrible to say the least, requiring him to help fellow Jews undress, direct them into the gas chambers, and remove the dead bodies after the event. Exaggeration is not the motivation behind this document. + Perhaps Bendel wanted to exonerate himself from having done the work of the Nazis by implying that he was made to do it. + Bendel probably wanted to make sure that those involved in the Final Solution received due punishment for their crimes.

Q3

Using the sources **and** your own knowledge, assess the impact of the SS and Gestapo on society in Nazi Germany.

Who were the SS and the Gestapo?

SS

The SS were formed as a branch of the SA in 1925, to act as Hitler's personal bodyguard. Led by Himmler from 1929, the SS began to develop into a racially selected, aristocratic elite, organised along medieval chivalric codes. With the motto of "Blood and Soil", the SS sought to create a new order based on Himmler's occultist beliefs, while protecting the Aryan people from 'alien' elements. By 1939, the SS had some 240,000 members and had a military branch called the Waffen-SS. The Death's Head Formations branch of the SS organised and ran concentration camps, although their true nature was not disclosed to the public (Source 1).

Gestapo (Source 3)

Under the direct command of Heydrich, the Gestapo had been formed out of the old Prussian secret police. After Himmler unified the police forces of Germany in 1936, the Gestapo became the most important security agent of the state. Most importantly, the Gestapo could define the law of the nation. The popular image of the Gestapo is one of repression and terror, but, while this was a 'reality' by 1942, there were only 30,000 officers. This has led to the disturbing picture of a Gestapo, incapable of maintaining its workload alone, being supported by a consenting public. The Gestapo was largely a reactive organisation.

Impact

The impact on the Jewish community goes without saying (Source 2), with the deaths of over six million and the trauma for those who survived. On other ethnic communities, eg the gypsies, a similar fate occurred, with some 500,000 being executed at various concentration camps. With regard to the impact on the German population, it is believed that some 80% of denunciations were voluntary, leaving us with a terror regime upheld and supported by the people, leading to over one million imprisonments in concentration camps and 32,000 'legal' executions.

The Church

Source 1

By its determination to carry through the political and moral purging of our public life, the Government is creating and ensuring the preconditions for a truly deep and inward religious life ... The National Government sees in both Christian denominations the most important factors for the maintenance of our society. It will respect the agreements concluded between them and the states; their rights will not be touched ... The National Government will permit and guarantee to the Christian denominations the enjoyment of their due influence in schools and education.

Extract from a speech by Hitler to the Reichstag, 23 March 1933, stressing the government's recognition of the importance of the churches
J Noakes and G Pridham (eds), *Nazism 1919–1945, vol 1* (University of Exeter Press, 1998)

Source 2

We will have to deal with Christianity in a tougher way than hitherto. We must settle accounts with this Christianity, the greatest of plagues that could have happened to us in our history, which has weakened us in every conflict ... Today at Heydrich's funeral I intentionally expressed in my oration from my deepest conviction a belief in God, a belief in fate, in the ancient one as I called him – that is the old germanic word: Wralda ... we must once again be rooted in our ancestors and grandchildren, in this eternal chain and eternal sequence ... If we do not secure this moral foundation which is the deepest and best ... we will not be able to overcome Christianity ...

Extract from an address by Himmler to the top leadership of the SS, 9 June 1942, in which he describes his own religious beliefs
J Noakes and G Pridham (eds), *Nazism 1919–1945, vol 2* (University of Exeter Press, 2000)

> **Source 3**
>
> *The Nazi regime achieved only limited success in its religious policy; the churches were severely handicapped, but not destroyed. Equally, the churches failed as well, for in their concern to defend Christianity itself they failed to offer a moral lead to oppose such a monstrous regime … The churches did not come out in open defence of the Jews either in fear of government revenge or of alienating public opinion or because they regarded persecution of the Jews as proof of God's curse.*
>
> **From David Evans and Jane Jenkins, *Years of Weimar and the Third Reich* (Hodder Murray, 1999)**

Q1

Study Source 1. **How useful is it as evidence for a historian studying Nazi aims for the Church in the period 1933–39?**

Usefulness for the study of the Church	
Date/Context	Written on 23 March 1933, one day before the Enabling Act was passed, this source is extremely useful for a historian studying Nazi aims for the Church. Delivered at the beginning of the regime, this speech identifies targets for religion and therefore allows us to make judgements regarding Nazi success or failure.
Author	Any source by Hitler is vital in the understanding of the Third Reich, given the very nature of his 'authoritarian' power. Hitler's declaration can therefore be seen as being at the very heart of the National Socialists' ideology, and is consequently extremely useful.
Mode	Since the source takes the form of a speech, Hitler would obviously have thought very carefully about its content and rehearsed its delivery. The public nature of the content will allow us to understand just what Hitler wanted his listeners to believe.

Target audience	The target audience for the speech was the Reichstag and therefore, through the press, the public. It must be remembered that this Reichstag was not Nazi dominated, and still contained parties such as the Social Democratic Party and the Centre Party led by Hitler's vice-chancellor von Papen. The German Communist Party (KPD) were the only party not represented. Considering the 'mixed' audience and Hitler's political position, we can appreciate how difficult a speech concerning religion must have been, especially as Hitler knew the Enabling Act would be brought forward for voting the following day.
Tone/ Language	The speech by Hitler is positive in nature. He makes confident pledges to religious groupings regarding their standing, while establishing a moral grounding for the Nazis who would ensure "the preconditions for a truly deep and inward religious life". In an emotional aspect of life, Hitler leaves no doubt with his confident declarations.
Content	While Hitler does mention "political and moral purging", he immediately promises to establish the preconditions for a "religious life". Both Christian denominations are mentioned as being important for the "maintenance of our society", and he asserts that "their rights will not be touched".
Motive/ Purpose	It would be negligent on the part of any historian to ignore the fact that this speech was made only a day before the Enabling Act was due to be debated. In consideration of this it must also be remembered that Hitler and von Papen, leader of the Catholic Centre Party, had struck a deal – in return for the safeguarding of the Catholic Church, von Papen and his party would agree to the Enabling Act which would, in essence, end the power of the Reichstag. While this deal had already been secured, perhaps Hitler felt that von Papen needed further public 'securities'. While Hitler's open declaration in this source would appear to give a positive outlook on religion in the Third Reich, a closer reading reveals his true intentions for faith, in that he wanted it to be "truly deep and inward" and not in any way comparable with the importance of the state and the individual's responsibility to it.

Limitations	While useful, the document has some limitations regarding the Nazi aims for the Church in the period 1933–39. • The source deals only with Nazi 'aims' at the beginning of 1933, making no reference to the concordat agreement between the state and the Vatican on 20 July. • No mention is made of the new Confessional Church (which broke away from the Reich Church), which was concerned with state interference and false theology of the German Christians. • There is no mention of the pagan Faith Movement encouraged by the Nazis and especially the SS, which sought to replace Christianity.

Q2

Sources 1 and 2 provide different contemporary views on the place of Christianity within Nazi Germany. *How* and *why* do they differ?

How		
Themes	**Source 1**	**Source 2**
Date/Context	23 March 1933	9 June 1942
Author	Hitler	Himmler
Mode	Speech	Address
Target audience	The Reichstag/general public	Top leadership of the SS
Tone/Language	Uplifting for the Christian Church, reassuring, inclusive	Anti-Christian, destructive
Content	• Government creating conditions for a deep and inward religious life • Christian denominations as most important factors in maintenance of society	• Christianity to be dealt with in tough way • Christianity as greatest of all plagues that Germany has experienced

• Respect for Church • Christian Church influence in education to be permitted and guaranteed	• Germany weakened by Christianity • Himmler's belief in God called Wralda • Need for the SS to become rooted in family ties – this to become moral foundation as it is the deepest and best

Why		
Themes	**Source 1**	**Source 2**
Context	**Basic difference overview** The Nazis recognise the importance of the Christian Church and respect the agreements made with it. Context • When the Nazis came to power they had been viewed by some members of the Christian Church as being 'defenders' of the faith against the evils of Communism. • The Nazis also had a similar outlook to the Church, eg in traditional cultural values like the importance of family life. In the Lutheran Church, nationalism and respect for the state could be found.	**Basic difference overview** Himmler sees Christianity as the greatest of plagues. Wralda is God. Christianity must be overcome. Context • Himmler sought to create in his SS a pure, Aryan race, leading to the removal of 'alien' elements and the increasing of the selective breeding which would turn the SS into a racial elite. • Himmler believed himself to be the reincarnated Heinrich I (first King of the Germans who died in 936). Other concepts emerged from his firm belief in the occult.

	+ Anti-Semitism had also been a small feature of parts of the Christian medieval Church.	
Motive/Purpose	+ While Hitler had been brought up as a Catholic, his real beliefs were against the Church, and he sought its replacement. Christianity represented a weak, Jewish-based faith and a loyalty away from the state. + Hitler sought a strong, assertive Aryan faith, but as a skilled politician he knew he could not implement such a change too quickly. + Hitler tactfully made his initial dealings with the Church positive in an attempt to gain some control and support, with the ultimate aim of reducing their influence. + Source 1 is evidence of such tactical manoeuvrings.	+ Himmler's belief in Wralda would have been common knowledge to those in the SS. It is difficult to tell whether or not they held similar personal beliefs. + Himmler may have been attempting to 'preach' his gospel and convert his SS officers. There can be no doubt that the death of Heydrich affected him greatly, and perhaps he saw this moment as an opportunity to reassert his convictions. + Himmler and Hitler had been responsible for the establishment of a new 'SS Church' called the German Faith Movement where some SS officers had got married. This church was entirely pagan in theology. + Himmler's address was only to the top leadership of the SS, as his pagan beliefs would not have been well-received by the general public.

Q3

Using the sources *and* your own knowledge, assess how successfully the Nazis controlled religion in the period 1933–39.

What churches existed in Nazi Germany?

Pre-1933

Catholic – 32% of population, mainly in the south and west. Powerful in its own right. Had its own youth organisations and schools. Mainly represented by Centre (Z) Party.

Protestant – 58% of population, typically Lutheran and Calvinist. Organised separately in 28 state-based churches.

Nazi period

The Reich Church

+ New umbrella organisation for the **Protestant** Church

+ Hitler hoped this would 'coordinate' Protestantism into a unified, state-controlled Church, but it had the opposite effect and the Confessional Church broke away.

Confessional Church

+ Set up in 1934 against state interference and false theology of the new German Christian movement

German Christians

+ Radical, racially-based Protestantism

+ Adopting Nazi-style uniforms and salutes, they called for the removal of 'un-German' elements from the gospel.

German Faith Movement

+ Wanted to replace Christianity with a Nazi, pagan faith with pagan rituals

+ Remained a small sect (Source 2)

Key policies and their effects (Source 3)

Policy	Effect	
Creation of unified Reich Church (Source 1)	Failed – Confessional Church broke away	Increasingly radical options
Concordat agreement with the Pope (Source 1)	Initial success – *but* later criticism against infringement against the concordat	
Use German Christians to make Protestantism more Nazi	Provoked reaction and increased support for Confessional Church	
Undermine and reduce influence of Catholic Church	Public hostility	
German Faith Movement to replace Christianity	Limited – postponed until after war	

THE JEWS

Source 1

Action committees ... are to be formed for putting into effect the planned boycott of Jewish shops, Jewish goods ... and Jewish lawyers ... The boycott is purely a defensive measure aimed exclusively against German Jewry.

The action committees must at once popularise the boycott by means of propaganda and enlightenment. The principle is: No German must any longer buy from a Jew or let him and his backers promote their goods ... It must be supported by the whole German people and must hit Jewry where it is most vulnerable ...

Extract from the order for the nationwide boycott of Jewish shops and businesses, issued on 29 March 1933 by a committee of Nazi hardliners headed by Julius Streicher, the hugely anti-Semitic Gauleiter of Franconia and editor of the anti-Semitic *Der Stürmer* ('The Attacker') newspaper
J Noakes and G Pridham (eds), *Nazism 1919–1945, vol 2* (University of Exeter Press, 2000)

Source 2

The 'final solution' of the Jewish question meant the complete extermination of Jews in Europe. I was ordered to establish extermination facilities at Auschwitz in June 1941 ... I visited Treblinka to find out how they carried out their extermination. The Camp Commandant told me that he had liquidated 80,000 in the course of one half year.

Extract from the testimony of Rudolph Hoess, camp commandant of Auschwitz extermination camp, at the International Military Tribunal, Nuremberg, 1945
International Military Tribunal, Nuremberg 1947–1949 (ND/1918–PS)

> **Source 3**
>
> *The Jewish laws are not taken very seriously because the population has other problems on its mind and is mostly of the opinion that the whole fuss about the Jews is only being made to divert people's attention from other things and to provide the SA with something to do ... [but] there are enough people who are influenced by the defamation of the Jews and regard the Jews as the originators of many bad things.*
>
> **Extract from a report by a Social Democrat contact inside Nazi Germany, for the SOPADE Executive Committee in Prague, September 1935**
> **J Noakes and G Pridham (eds), *Nazism 1919–1945, vol 2* (University of Exeter Press, 2000)**

Q1

Study Source 1. How useful is it as evidence for a historian studying Nazi persecution of the Jews?

Usefulness for the study of the Jews	
Date/ Context	Issued at the beginning of the Nazi era, this document is very useful regarding the persecution of the Jews. This order is the first 'official', public action taken against the Jewish community by the Nazi government, setting the tone for the making of further laws.
Author	It is unlikely that Julius Streicher penned this document in isolation from Hitler, as it was such a controversial policy. While the committee would have developed the finer details, it is probable that this law was devised by the Nazi hierarchy.
Mode	In the form of an order, this boycott was given the weight of national law and is therefore useful in understanding Nazi persecution of the Jews. While 'ground violence' by the SA towards the Jews was commonplace in urban communities early in 1933, this remained unsanctioned by the government.
Target audience	The target audience is split into two major groups – the action committees, whose task it was to establish the boycott, and the general public, who would have been affected by it. Again, this is useful because the persecution of the Jews on this occasion was in full view of the public and was not being executed in secret.

Tone/ Language	As this is an order, the tone is informative and commanding. The phrase "Action committees … *are* to be formed" leaves us in no doubt that these are not optional and that their "planned" activities must happen "at once" and "must be supported".
Content	As this is the first of many state initiatives against the Jews, the content is of particular value regarding their persecution. We learn that action committees are to be formed and that the boycott is essentially economic in nature, being against Jewish shops and goods. While it is claimed in the source that the action is "purely a defensive measure", there is an obvious concern that it might not be seen that way, hence the need to "popularise the boycott by means of propaganda and enlightenment". While the boycott is to be made public, it is unlikely the final section of the source is meant for the public's eyes, with phrases like "It must be supported by the whole German people and must hit Jewry where it is most vulnerable". A more probable interpretation of this line is that it is meant to ensure the newly-formed committees understand the importance of their new-found task.
Motive/ Purpose	Having secured a great deal of power under the Enabling Act on 24 March 1933, Hitler, under pressure from local Nazi bosses, gave way to state-sanctioned persecution of the Jews. While Hitler was hugely anti-Semitic, he was clever enough to realise his need to consolidate the power of his party and his own personal power. While increasingly radical in policy and deed towards the Jews throughout the Third Reich, Hitler only took limited action against them initially as his need to improve the economy was paramount to win the support of the people. This boycott, while Hitler was personally in favour, was a great risk to his own authority and reputation, not only within the party and state, but also abroad. Perhaps this is why propaganda and enlightenment are seen as necessary to "popularise" the boycott – reputation was everything.

Limitations	While the source has many uses, it is extremely limited for the study of Nazi policies towards the Jews as it fails to mention: • the SA and increasing 'ground violence' up to 1935 • the Nuremberg Laws of 1935 • the Night of Broken Glass, 1938 • the creation of ghettoes • the extensive use of concentration camps and slave labour • the Wannsee Conference and the introduction of the Final Solution, implemented by the SS

Q2

Sources 1 and 2 provide different contemporary accounts of Nazi methods of Jewish persecution. *How* and *why* do they differ?

How		
Themes	**Source 1**	**Source 2**
Date/Context	29 March 1933	1945
Author	Nazi Party officials	Rudolph Hoess, camp commandant of Auschwitz
Mode	Order/Law	Testimony
Target audience	Action committees and later general public	International Military Tribunal at Nuremberg
Tone/Language	Commanding and forceful	Toneless, appears devoid of emotion
Content	• Action committees to put in place a boycott in Germany • Boycott to be popularised by propaganda and enlightenment • Must be supported by German people and hit Jewry where most vulnerable	• Complete extermination of the Jews in Europe • Hoess ordered to establish extermination facilities at Auschwitz • Liquidation of 80,000 Jews at Treblinka in the course of six months

Why		
Themes	**Source 1**	**Source 2**
Context	**Basic difference overview** Actions against the Jews are low-key, public and only directed against the economic aspect of Jewish life in Germany– no Jew was killed as a result of the boycott. **Context** ♦ Hitler's anti-Semitism featured heavily in *Mein Kampf* and the Secret Book. ♦ While only 14% of those who voted Nazi in 1932 did so for anti-Semitic reasons, they were widely known for holding this belief. ♦ Hardline Nazi bosses had been calling for government approved action against the Jews since Hitler had become chancellor. Hitler had refused as he was worried about a potential public backlash.	**Basic difference overview** Actions against the Jews are secret and fatal and directed against the entire Jewish community in Europe. **Context** ♦ Nazi persecution of the Jews reached new heights from the beginning of the war. After the defeat of Poland, concentration camps multiplied weekly and the SS slave labour system developed rapidly utilising the approximately two million Jews living there. ♦ 'Killing squads' or Einzatsgruppen had travelled throughout Poland from village to village, rounding up local Jews and executing them at gunpoint. ♦ Ghettoes became regular scenes of death mainly caused by starvation and disease.

		• Himmler became worried about the effects of daily executions on his SS men. New ways were sought to kill Jews quickly and en masse. • Wannsee Conference led by Reinhard Heydrich organised the Final Solution of all Jews within Europe
Motive/Purpose	• The boycott was designed to hurt the Jews economically for a limited period of time, but not to the extent of damaging the German economy, which was very fragile as a result of the Great Depression. • Hitler was obviously concerned about public opinion, as we can see from the inclusion of the phrase "popularise the boycott by means of propaganda and enlightenment". This phraseology reflects the newly-established Ministry for Public Enlightenment and Propaganda on 13 March under the leadership of Goebbels. • The order was the first 'legal' action taken against the Jews. This order took some of the pressure off Hitler from Nazi officials in lower ranks of the party.	• Hoess' statement to the International Military Tribunal at Nuremberg had no ulterior motive. Rather, it was a simple statement of fact. • Hoess knew that there was no way he would escape justice and therefore had no reason to lie. • Hoess' testimony as a whole contained little that could be construed as an apology for his actions at Auschwitz. As this extract shows, there is nothing 'emotional' in tone or phrase. • It could be suggested from this extract that Hoess was trying to pass the blame for his actions by stating "I was ordered".

Q3

Using the sources *and* your own knowledge, assess the impact of Nazi policies towards the Jews in the period 1933–45.

What were Nazi policies towards the Jews?

1933: One-day boycott against Jewish shops/businesses and lawyers (April) (Source 1). Originally this boycott was to run for three weeks. Due to international pressure, especially from the US, the boycott was reduced to three days. Once in operation, it proved unsuccessful as many Germans simply ignored the notices regarding the action and it was duly ended after one day. Hitler had fought against the boycott for a considerable time and had been worried about its consequences for the recovering economy, but he was never concerned about the welfare of those Jews affected.

1935: Law for the Protection of German Blood and German Honour; Reich Citizenship Law; Law for the Protection of the Genetic Health of the German People. These three laws in turn devastated the Jew by legal means. With 'mixed' marriages being forbidden, citizenship removed, and 'certificates of fitness' being issued for marriage, the German Jew had become a mirage. In essence, these laws had two major effects. Firstly they legalised the day-to-day intimidation by the SA of Jews in local communities throughout 1933 and 1934. This violence had seen countless Jews beaten to death or put into 'protective custody' and the suicide rate of young Jewish males rose at an alarming pace. Secondly, the laws drew a new line in the sand for Jewish persecution and intimidation of Jewish communities which were now state-sanctioned.

1938: Krystallnacht, Night of Broken Glass. After a fatal shooting of a Nazi official in Paris by a Jew, Goebbels unleashed his most 'dramatic' propaganda event to date, with a series of attacks on thousands of Jewish businesses and synagogues between 9–10 November. With some 91 Jews being murdered and between 20,000 to 30,000 deported to concentration camps, this very public display of anti-Semitism had far-reaching consequences. Goering, furious at the action due to it upsetting his Four Year Plan, charged the Jews one billion RM for the damage. However, Heydrich and the SD (Jewish department of the SS) took charge of all Jews in Germany. The fate of the Jew was now firmly in the hands of Himmler's racial elite.

1939: In January, Hitler announced to the Reichstag his intention to destroy European Jewry if it started another war. When war finally broke out in September, Einzatsgruppen murdered thousands in Poland and the SS moved hundreds of thousands into ghettoes.

1940: Madagascar. This was thought of by the Nazis as a location for some four million Jews, but the plan never left the drawing board.

1941: Mass murder. Russia was invaded and 500,000 Jews were shot. Between July and October a decision was finally taken on the Final Solution, with gassing of Jewish prisoners taking place at some camps.

1942: The Final Solution was organised at the Wannsee Conference by Heydrich. 11 million European Jews were identified and labelled for extermination. By 1943 the extermination camp system was extended by Himmler to accommodate this decision. (Source 2)

1945: Six million Jews were dead.

Impact of policies?

Clearly the Jewish population was not under any mortal threat from the majority of German citizens in the early Nazi period (Source 3). However, the Jewish community came under increasing, state-sanctioned, legal 'terror' by 1935, added to by ruthless 'unofficial' fanatical anti-Semites such as the SA. By 1938, those Jews who could left the country in order to escape the growing violence and racial discrimination, but by 1939 the door was largely closed. During the war, the fanatics of the Nazi Party, including Hitler himself, came to see that the Jewish problem could never be fixed by resettlement to another country. 'Resettlement' to a mass grave was more appealing.

Ultimately, Nazi policies resulted in the ruthless and systematic destruction of six million Jews.

Youth

Source 1

And the Führer demands of you and of us all that we train ourselves to a life of service and duty, of loyalty and comradeship. You, ten-year-old cub, and you, lass, are not too young nor too small to practise obedience and discipline, to integrate yourself into the community and show yourself to be a comrade. Like you, millions of young Germans are today swearing allegiance to the Führer and it is a proud picture of unity which German youth today presents to the whole world. So today you make a vow to your Führer and here, before your parents, the Party and your comrades, we now receive you into our great community of loyalty. Your motto will always be:
'Fuhrer, command — we follow!'

Extract from an oath which members of the Hitler Youth were required to swear for admission to the DJ (Deutsches Jungvolk – German Young People), dated April 1940
J Noakes and G Pridham (eds), *Nazism 1919–1945, vol 2* (University of Exeter Press, 2000)

Source 2

The day of reckoning has come, the day when German youth will settle accounts with the vilest tyranny ever endured by our nation. In the name of German youth, we demand from Adolf Hitler's state the restoration of personal freedom ...

We grew up in a state where every free expression of opinion has been ruthlessly suppressed ...

There can be but one word of action for us: Fight the party! Quit the party organisations, where all discussion is now being stifled ... Each of us must join in the fight for our future, for a life in freedom and honour in a state that is aware of its moral obligations ...

Extract from a pamphlet distributed to the public by the White Rose group (an anti-Nazi Youth organisation) in Munich, 18 February 1943

Source 3

The direct pressures on teachers to teach the line of Nazi ideology in almost every sphere and aspect showed itself outwardly in a gradual replacement of history books and a methodical introduction of portraits of the Führer and paintings of battle scenes and such like. Schools became little more than Nazi training institutes, where German youth were prepared for their eventual role in the ensuing war.

From Henry Metelmann, *A Hitler Youth: Growing up in Germany in the 1930s* (Spellmount Publishers, 2004)
Metelmann was born in 1922 and joined the Hitler Youth at the age of 12, becoming increasingly involved in the Nazi movement.

Q1

Study Source 1. How useful is it as evidence for a historian studying the aims of Nazi youth policy?

Usefulness for the study of youth	
Date/Context	Dated April 1940, this contemporary source is very useful for understanding the aims of Nazi youth policy. Written during the Third Reich and during the Second World War, this source can give us an unmistakable insight into the desires of Nazi youth leaders for their young charges.
Author	While no specific author is mentioned, someone from the party, perhaps even Baldur von Schirach himself, would have devised this oath. As the Nazis held youth in high esteem, it would seem reasonable to suggest that this oath would, in every way, have reflected core National Socialist ideology.
Mode	As an oath, this source is of great use to a historian. The promises made via this document show us just how seriously the Nazis took youth policies, and just how much they desired the integration of young people into the Volk.

Target audience	The target audience is primarily the young people who are swearing the oath. Such a ceremony, as we read from the source, took place in full view of parents, guardians and friends, making the oath a potent reminder to the adults that their children were servants of the Führer and were under his command.
Tone/ Language	The language is as you would expect in an oath, with words such as "demands", "duty", "loyalty", and "comradeship", followed by "obedience" and "discipline". With a clear command at the end, this oath is, without doubt, a very serious affair.
Content	This oath leaves nothing to chance in the life of a young person. Reading more like an oath for entrance into the army, 10–14-year-old boys and girls in essence swore their lives away to the Führer and became integrated into the community of National Socialism. According to the source, children "are not too young nor too small", leaving us as historians in no doubt as to just how important young people were to the Nazi Party.
Motive/ Purpose	As suggested earlier, the oath is not simply a pledge which young people were expected to make for entrance into an organisation. This oath operated at a much deeper, ideological level and was taken very seriously by those Nazi officials in charge of the groups. While evidently also taken seriously by some of the boys and girls, it served largely as a potent reminder to parents that the Führer was in control and that the community was of paramount importance. While the oath is clearly adult in nature, it is quite possible that this was purposely done to enhance the importance of the occasion and to elevate the young person to a proxy adulthood.
Limitations	While this source is extremely useful, it does have its limitations regarding the aims of Nazi youth policy. • It was written in 1940, seven years after the Nazis had come to power, and therefore it cannot reflect the aims previously set by Hitler.

	• It makes no reference to other organisations within the Hitler Youth and the goals of each section.
	• No reference is made to education within the Third Reich, and its role in the indoctrination process.
	• No distinction is made between the boys (who were to be like soldiers) and girls (who were to get married and have as many children as possible), which is vital to any historian studying Nazi aims.
	• No mention is made of the importance of race and eugenics in youth education.

Q2

Sources 1 and 2 provide different contemporary obligations for the youth of Nazi Germany. How and why do they differ?

How		
Themes	**Source 1**	**Source 2**
Date/Context	April 1940	18 February 1943
Author	Nazi Party	White Rose group
Mode	Oath	Pamphlet
Target audience	Boys and girls/parents	General public
Tone/Language	Commanding, demanding, serious	Dramatic and outspoken, defiant against the Nazi Party
Content	• Boys and girls to train themselves in a life of duty, loyalty and comradeship • Youth to practise obedience and discipline	• Youth will settle accounts with the vilest tyranny ever endured. • Free expression of opinion has been ruthlessly suppressed.

	• Youth received into the community of loyalty • Motto to always be "Fuhrer command – we follow!"	• Youth should fight the party and quit the organisations. • All must fight for the future, for a life in freedom and honour.

Why		
Themes	**Source 1**	**Source 2**
Context	**Basic difference overview** The oath places high demands of loyalty and obedience to Hitler and the state. **Context** • The main thrust of Nazi ideology was focused on the youth of Germany. Indoctrination via school education or the Hitler Youth Movement was vital for the future of National Socialism and the Third Reich. • The Hitler Youth Movement, headed by Baldur von Schirach, began with boys aged from 6–18 years, while the girls joined at 10 and carried on until 21.	**Basic difference overview** The freedoms of youth have been suppressed and they must fight against the state. **Context** • While membership of any youth organisation except the Hitler Youth was banned in 1936, many young people detested the growing political and ideological bias of the Nazi programme. • 'Alternative', illegal youth movements formed, such as the Edelweiss Pirates, Navajos, and Swing. • Their aims were uncertain. Many simply wanted to stay away from the intrusive Nazi state.

		During the war, many of the peace-loving movements, like the White Rose, became increasingly involved in pro-active anti-Nazi resistance, in some cases resulting in death by hanging or deportation to concentration camps.
Motive/ Purpose	• This oath was designed and used to reflect National Socialist aims for all German youth, especially obedience to and love of the Führer. • The oath reflected all propaganda present in Germany since 1933 and thereby reinforced Nazi principles. • The oath also served as a reminder to parents of what was expected of their children in the Third Reich, as well as of what was expected of themselves.	• This pamphlet aims to awaken a spirit of rebellion, especially among the youth, against the Nazi state. • The timing of the document is important as, by 1943, the German army had begun to suffer defeats at the hands of the Russians. • Using such words as "freedom", "moral" and "suppressed" would have hit a nerve among many individuals by 1943, as failures in war reflected the growing problems on the home front.

Q3

Using the sources *and* your own knowledge, assess the impact of Nazi policies on the youth of Nazi Germany in the period 1933–39.

What were Nazi youth policies?

In essence, youth policies can be found in two major areas – firstly via **organisations**, secondly via **education**.

Nazi organisations for German youth

Boys: Cubs (6–10)   Girls: Young Girls (10–14)
       Young German Boys (10–14)   League of German Girls (14–18)
       Hitler Youth (14–18)   Faith and Beauty (18–21)

Fun and excitement were the order of the day in the Hitler Youth. Activities such as sports, youth rallies, hikes, weekend camps and military-style games were commonplace. However, the Hitler Youth was essentially a 'young army'. Intimidation, constant reminders of their duty to the Führer (Source 1), and the increasingly serious atmosphere led many young people to keep away from the organisation, even when it became compulsory.

Education

+ The Nazi Party extended control over schools by coordinating teachers into the National Socialist Teachers' League (NSLB). By 1937, 97% of teachers had joined, pressurised or not. All teachers had to attend one-month training courses which stressed Nazi ideology and PE.

+ The curriculum was changed (Source 3), with PE, History and Biology being heavily adapted to National Socialist thinking. By 1935 all textbooks had to be approved before use. Boys and girls also took on different classes which reflected Nazi thinking, eg girls did needlework and home crafts.

+ Adolf Hitler Schools were established in 1937 by Schirach and Robert Ley, as centres of elite leadership training, although in effect they were limited in number and influence.

+ NAPOLAs (established in 1933) were similar to Adolf Hitler Schools, although they were also limited in effectiveness and support.

+ Castles of Order or 'Ordensburgen' were finishing schools for the military and political elite, although these were for 25–30 year olds.

+ Higher education remained largely untouched academically, although numbers were greatly diminished between 1933–39 – by around 50%. Lecturers were required to join the Nazi Lecturers' Association and students the German Students' League.

Indoctrination

The Nazis sought to indoctrinate the youth of Germany. Core values included:

+ obedience
+ idolising the Führer
+ self-sacrifice for the national good
+ strengthening the health and racial purity of the German nation
+ being physically fit
+ fighting for Germany (boy)
+ bearing many children (girl)

Impact?

This is hard to measure accurately. Many young people in Germany were capable of independent thinking, but it would have been increasingly difficult for any young person going to school and attending a Nazi organisation such as the Hitler Youth not to be affected in some way. A Wilt (*Nazi Germany*, 1994) suggests that 95% of German young people backed the Nazis (or Hitler at least). However, not all German youth 'fell under the spell' of the Nazis.

Opposition

While German young people had no control over their school curriculum, some, as suggested earlier, did not join Nazi organisations. While small in number, groups like the Edelweiss Pirates and the White Rose (Source 2) identified with each other simply through their nonconformity to the rules laid down by the state. While an annoyance for the party, the Gestapo did not aggressively disband these groups until the war was well under way, and only then because these anti-Nazi youth movements enlisted in the resistance movement.

Conclusion

By 1939, many young people in Germany knew nothing except Nazi ideology and Hitler. For many it was fun, dynamic and exciting, with a great sense of camaraderie and community. There were however, although few, some young people who did not support the regime and would eventually die in attempting to bring it down.

A2: The partition of Ireland 1900–1925

REASONS FOR OPPOSITION TO HOME RULE

Source 1

We, Irishmen belonging to the three southern provinces … protest against the creation of an Executive dependent for its existence upon the pleasure of such a Parliament. We do so upon the following grounds:– Because any measure for the creation of a separate Irish Parliament and a separate Irish Executive would produce most dangerous social confusion, involving a disastrous conflict of interests and classes, and a serious risk of civil war …

Because such a measure would imperil personal liberty, freedom of opinion, and the spirit of tolerance in Ireland;

Because such a measure, instead of effecting a settlement, would inevitably pave the way for further efforts towards the complete separation of Ireland and Great Britain;

Because no statutory limitations restricting the authority of an Irish Legislative Assembly or the power of an Irish Executive could protect the freedom and the rights of minorities in this country;

Because such a measure would hand over Ireland to the government of a party which … had proved itself … unworthy of the exercise of power by its repeated defiance of the law …

Finally, regarding the question from a wider point of view than that which concerns alone the internal government of Ireland, highly prizing as we do the advantages we derive from our present imperial position, and being justly proud of the place we Irishmen have long held amongst those to whom the Empire owes its prosperity and fame, having been always faithful in our allegiance to our Sovereigns and upholders of the Constitution, we protest against any change that will deprive us of our birthright, by which we stand on equal ground with our fellow-countrymen of Great Britain as subjects of our King and citizens of the British Empire.

Extract from a declaration adopted by Southern Unionists at a meeting in Dublin, 10 October 1911
Published in the English press, 11 October 1911

Source 2

In our opposition ... we shall not be guided by the considerations or bound by the restraints which would influence us in an ordinary constitutional struggle ... They may, perhaps they will, carry their home rule bill through the House of Commons, but what then? I said the other day in the House of Commons and I repeat here that there are things stronger than parliamentary majorities.

... Before I occupied the position I now fill in the party I said that, in my belief, if an attempt were made to deprive these men [Ulster Unionists] of their birth-right — as part of a corrupt parliamentary bargain — they would be justified in resisting such an attempt by all means in their power, including force. I said it then, and I repeat it now with a full sense of the responsibility which attaches to my position, that, in my opinion, if such an attempt is made, I can imagine no length of resistance to which Ulster can go in which I should not be prepared to support them, and in which, in my belief, they would not be supported by the overwhelming majority of the British people.

Extract from Bonar Law's address to a mass meeting in the grounds of Blenheim Palace
Published in the English press, 29 July 1912

Source 3

Being convinced in our consciences that Home Rule would be disastrous to the material well-being of Ulster, as well as of the whole of Ireland, subversive of our civil and religious freedom, destructive of our citizenship, and perilous to the unity of the Empire, we, whose names are underwritten, men of Ulster, loyal subjects of His Gracious Majesty King George V, humbly relying on the God Whom our fathers in the days of stress and trial confidently trusted, do hereby pledge ourselves in solemn Covenant throughout this our time of threatened calamity to stand by one another in defending for ourselves and our children our cherished position of equal citizenship in the United Kingdom and in using all means which may be found necessary to defeat the present conspiracy to set up a home rule parliament in Ireland. And in the event of such a Parliament being forced upon us we further and mutually pledge ourselves to refuse to recognise its authority. In sure confidence that God will defend the right, we hereto subscribe our names. And further we individually declare that we have not already signed this Covenant. God Save the King.

Ulster's Solemn League and Covenant
Published in the English press, 20 September 1912

Q1

Consult Sources 1 and 3. Explain and compare the views taken by the Southern Unionists and Ulster Unionists on the Home Rule issue.

Source 1 outlines the Southern Unionist position in October 1911, just after the passage of the Parliament Act, which had made the success of a new Home Rule Bill more likely. Clearly they were concerned about their security, particularly when they believed that the implementation of Home Rule might provoke a civil war. Similarly, Southern Unionists were also worried about their minority status, believing that no matter what legislative safeguards were devised there would be no real protection for them under Home Rule.

Like Ulster Unionists, Southern Unionists were convinced that the implementation of Home Rule would be the first step on the road to complete separation for Ireland. This fear had existed since the Parnell era, when the IPP was often vague about its ultimate aim. However, Source 1 conveys the sense of outrage among Southern Unionists at the prospect of their former agrarian tormentors assuming control of a new Irish government. Their opinion was that law-breakers could not become law-makers, and they identified a number of leading figures in the IPP such as John Dillon, who had been heavily involved in various agrarian campaigns in the last quarter of the nineteenth century. As Alvin Jackson has emphasised, Irish Unionism in general, and Southern Unionism in particular, had from the outset made the defence of landlordism a prominent feature of its programme. This reflected the differing social classes within the two strands of Unionism. While Ulster Unionism consisted of a cross-class alliance, the landlord class was the dominant force in Southern Unionism. The final paragraph illustrates the broader view that was consistently taken by Southern Unionists, who had genuine concerns about the detrimental effect which Home Rule might have on the Empire. While Ulster Unionists make reference to the Empire in Source 3, it is clear that Southern Unionists, as Patrick Buckland has argued, were more closely integrated with Conservatives on the mainland (British Unionists) and that they shared many of their wider concerns.

This, of course, contrasts with the more parochial attitude of the Ulster Unionists which can be gleaned from reading Source 3, the Solemn League and Covenant. In this famous document there is a clear focus on Ulster, and the religious objection to Home Rule articulated by many Ulster Unionist leaders is prominently featured. Indeed, the Covenant has a powerful religious undertone throughout, and it is written in Old Testament-style language. The Ulstermen were putting their trust in God in their hour of need, suggesting as Joe Lee has claimed that Ulster Unionists drew parallels with the ancient Israelites escaping from persecution in Egypt. Not surprisingly, in view of Ulster's industrial success in the nineteenth century, there is a brief reference to the threat that Home Rule might pose to Ulster's economic prosperity, but the objections to Home Rule outlined in the Covenant are primarily religious, not economic.

If the emphasis on the religious objection to Home Rule helps us to distinguish between the Southern Unionist and Ulster Unionist approaches to Home Rule, then the reference to the use of "all means which may be found necessary" to resist Home Rule, which many observers took to mean violence, provides another key difference in strategy. Their sheer weight of numbers allowed Ulster Unionists to consider alternatives that were simply not available to their colleagues in the South. There was, moreover, a direct link between the Covenant and the formation of the UVF a few months later. Equally significant, however, was the prospect of passive resistance on a grand scale if the British government sought to impose Home Rule on Ulster. In their opposition to Home Rule Ulster Unionists shared the Conservative view that Asquith's Liberal government was acting unconstitutionally, since the Liberals had not made Home Rule for Ireland a specific manifesto commitment in either of the two general elections of 1910. Of course, the Covenant's reference to a "conspiracy", resulting from what Ulster Unionists felt was an underhand deal between the Liberals and Irish Nationalists, was illogical, but there was little doubt that the sense of outrage felt by all shades of Unionism was genuine. Overall, the two sources highlight the essential differences between Southern Unionists and Ulster Unionists both in terms of their respective reasons for opposing Home Rule and the contrasting strategies adopted by each strand in the struggle against it.

Q2

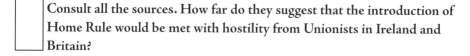

Consult all the sources. How far do they suggest that the introduction of Home Rule would be met with hostility from Unionists in Ireland and Britain?

While the Southern Unionists emphasise in Source 1 that the implementation of Home Rule could result in civil war, there is no specific reference to the role that they would play in such a conflict. This merely reflects the weakness of Southern Unionists. Their lack of numbers, approximately ten per cent in the three Southern provinces, meant not only that the prospect of armed resistance was out of the question but also that the use of violent rhetoric was likely to be counterproductive. Southern Unionists recognised their limitations, but their feeling of insecurity, which Source 1 highlights, did not mean that they would be nervous spectators in the struggle against Home Rule. Instead, as Patrick Buckland has documented, they threw their energy into an anti-Home Rule propaganda blitz on the mainland, using their wealth and their connections in Britain to useful effect.

As Source 2 indicates, Andrew Bonar Law, who had become leader of the Conservative Party in November 1911, clearly did not share these inhibitions. His speech to 13,000 Unionist supporters in the grounds of Blenheim Palace, an Oxfordshire estate, at the end of July 1912 appears to be unequivocal on the use of violence. Bonar Law states that his party would disregard the sovereignty of parliament if Home Rule was enacted and would support any means of resistance employed by the Ulstermen. He justifies the use of violence by arguing that as the Liberal government's actions were unconstitutional, then it must follow that Unionist reaction would be unconstitutional. Not surprisingly, Bonar Law's Blenheim speech created an outcry in the Liberal press, where his warning that there were "things stronger than parliamentary majorities" was described as wild and inflammatory and a throwback to the upheaval of the English Revolution in the mid-seventeenth century. Yet Bonar Law's speech has to be read in context. At the time each of the four main parties – Liberal, Conservative, Nationalist and Unionist – were increasing the rhetoric, and Bonar Law's Blenheim speech was a direct response to an Asquith address in Dublin on the previous weekend, when the Prime Minister poured scorn on Unionist threats of a civil war. It is also true that in resorting to such violent language Bonar Law was reflecting the sense of desperation felt by the Conservative Party which, having lost three general elections in succession, was desperate for power. Bonar Law himself was still finding his feet as party leader, and he was determined to carry the fight to his Liberal opponents, adopting a much more confrontational approach than his predecessor, Arthur Belfour. However, as Paul Bew has noted, Bonar Law was more moderate in private than his public speeches suggested. Unlike other leading Tories, such as Walter Long, he was never against Irish self-government but was keen to safeguard Ulster's position in the United Kingdom. While his Blenheim speech suggests that Home Rule would be met by hostility, it can to some extent be seen as part of the ongoing campaign of rhetoric indulged in by Edward Carson, James Craig and the rest of the Unionist leadership. Clearly, it predates the formation of the UVF, but, as Nicholas Mansergh has suggested, Bonar Law's stance gave vital support to the Ulster Unionist campaign of resistance and probably encouraged the leadership to adopt an extremist strategy. As the events of March 1914 later demonstrated, Bonar Law had no qualms about immobilising the British Army in order to strengthen the Unionist position. Yet it should also be noted that the Blenheim speech caused apprehension among some leading Conservatives, so the prospect of unqualified Conservative support for any armed action taken by the Ulster Unionists was by no means guaranteed.

107

The Covenant catches what ATQ Stewart has described as the mood of grim determination in the North, and there is a suggestion that if all constitutional means fail then armed resistance to Home Rule would be inevitable. There was, moreover, a direct link between the Covenant and the UVF as only those who had signed the Covenant were initially eligible to join the new paramilitary group. On the other hand, the more likely response to the introduction of Home Rule was, as Source 3 suggests, a province-wide campaign of passive resistance, as Unionists would refuse to recognise the authority of any new Dublin parliament. This made more sense, as the Unionists in the North, certainly at that stage, did not have the capacity to contemplate armed resistance. As Alvin Jackson has explained, Carson may have threatened violence but, ultimately, he regarded such a course as suicidal. This makes it possible to understand the wider context of the Solemn League and Covenant. Not only was it a masterful propaganda stroke meticulously planned by Craig, but it was also a clear attempt to discipline the Unionist rank and file which had shown signs of losing control during the summer of 1912. In particular, Carson had been embarrassed by the expulsion of Catholic workers from the shipyard, and he was acutely aware that his extra-parliamentary strategy would not bear fruit unless he maintained a firm grip on his followers in the North. It can be concluded, therefore, that while the establishment of a Home Rule parliament in Dublin would have sparked some violence, this would probably have been isolated and sporadic as the leadership sought to implement its strategy of passive resistance.

While Sources 2 and 3 make direct references to armed resistance, much of this was for propaganda purposes, and there was a clear recognition between both the Conservative and Ulster Unionist leaderships that violence could indeed be counterproductive.

Q3

Consult all the sources. Which of them would a historian value most in a study of the nature of Unionist resistance to Home Rule?

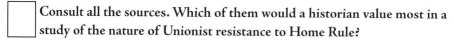

Taken together, the three sources offer an insight into the different perspectives of British and Irish Unionists in their struggle against Home Rule.

Source 1 lists the reasons for Southern Unionist opposition to Home Rule. These reflect the broader view taken by Southern Unionists, some of whom had family links and business interests in England. In addition to their concerns about the future of the United Kingdom and the Empire, however, there is a clear reference to the social chaos which they anticipated following the establishment of a Home Rule parliament. Southern Unionists were, at this time, desperately trying to defend their privileged position at the top of Irish society, and they were alarmed at the prospect of power passing to a party that was dominated by their radical agrarian opponents. An obvious weakness of the source is that there is no reference to the strategy that Southern Unionists might adopt in their struggle against Home Rule. There is some indication of their sense of insecurity, but no explanation is offered as to how they might overcome their numerical weakness, nor is there any mention of an intention to combine with their fellow Unionists in the North in order to combat the Home Rule threat. More specifically, there is no reference to their ongoing propaganda drive on the mainland, where they sought to influence voters in key marginal constituencies.

Source 2 conveys the support given to Unionists by the Conservative Party, and it records Bonar Law's personal commitment to the Ulster cause. Bonar Law's Ulster Presbyterian roots and his ability to empathise with Unionists in the North naturally brought a new dimension to the Home Rule crisis. It is very doubtful if any other Conservative leader would have pursued such an extreme course or used such militant rhetoric. Bonar Law cared passionately about Ulster, and he justified his extremist stance by arguing that Home Rule was a consequence of the "corrupt parliamentary bargain" made by the Liberals and Irish Nationalists. The Blenheim speech is particularly useful because Bonar Law specifies the use of "force" and in so doing he associates himself unequivocally with the armed resistance being planned by the Ulster Unionist leadership. Source 2 also demonstrates Bonar Law's attempts to raise the political stakes and force the government's hand. While his personal commitment to the Ulster cause was never in doubt, Bonar Law was also aware of the wider benefits for his party as it recovered from the damaging splits over tariff reform and the Lords' veto. Forceful opposition to Home Rule served his purpose of uniting the party while exploiting an obvious weakness in his Liberal opponents. There was, moreover, a great deal of lingering bitterness between the parties caused by the furore over the Parliament Act, and Bonar Law's leadership style was to seize every opportunity which might create difficulties for the Liberal government. It is also true that Bonar Law's speech unnerved a number of leading Conservatives who were perturbed by what they regarded as his irresponsible language. Nevertheless, Source 2 is an invaluable example of the Conservative Party's support for Ulster resistance to Home Rule and of its leader's personal commitment. It shows the anger and frustration felt by Bonar Law, who was working on the basis that normal parliamentary politics had been suspended as a result of the government's refusal to hold an election on the Home Rule issue. His most recent biographer, RJQ Adams, has suggested that the Blenheim speech should be interpreted as part of his underlying strategy to force the Prime Minister to choose between a general election and resistance.

Source 3 captures the deep sense of betrayal felt by Ulster Unionists in 1912. The Third Home Rule Bill was making its way through parliament and the government had emphasised that concessions would not be considered. Unionists in Ulster viewed the Liberal plans as a "conspiracy", and this determined their unconstitutional approach. Accordingly, signatories of the Covenant could profess loyalty to the King while simultaneously engaging in menacing defiance of his government. Source 3 also helps our understanding of the Unionist leadership's preoccupation with the need to impose much tighter discipline on their supporters following the occurrence of serious sectarian incidents in the summer of 1912. While the Covenant emphasises unity of purpose and action, it also highlights the desirability of a highly disciplined mass movement, and this was to play a central role in Ulster Unionism's extra-parliamentary resistance to Home Rule. The Covenant became the centrepiece of a week's activity of events and Unionist rallies, which served its purpose of mobilising support in Ulster and restoring discipline among the rank and file. It also attracted huge press coverage in England where there was a new emphasis on the fierce determination of Ulster Unionists to reject Home Rule. Although it was primarily a propaganda exercise, the Covenant clearly illustrates the importance of the religious objection to Home Rule which dominated Ulster Unionist thinking. Paul Bew has analysed the impact of the *Ne Temere* decree in Ulster which, together with the McCann case, had raised sectarian tension in the province in the years immediately preceding the introduction of the Third Home Rule Bill. For rank-and-file Unionists in the North the defence of their religious liberty was of fundamental importance in their rejection of Home Rule for Ireland, and Source 3 is particularly useful in emphasising the strength of this religious feeling. Moreover, the Covenant outlines the possibilities open to Ulster Unionists in their campaign of resistance to Home Rule. Any attempt to impose a Home Rule parliament in Ireland would be met with passive resistance, and there was a real possibility that armed resistance would be organised.

Strong arguments could be advanced for both Sources 2 and 3 being valuable to a historian studying the nature of Unionist resistance to Home Rule, but Source 3 is more wide-ranging in its assessment.

Strategies for opposition to Home Rule

Source 1

Sir – In the present crisis in the history of our country the position of the loyalists in the South and West of Ireland is, I fear, somewhat overlooked by the people of Great Britain. It seems to be largely assumed that in the Southern and Western provinces hostility to the Home Rule Bill is either non-existent or so insignificant as to be unworthy of consideration.

Probably the reason for this erroneous impression is to be found in the fact that the determination of Ulster to resist Home Rule by physical force has to a large extent overshadowed all other considerations.

But, in truth, the opposition of the loyal population outside of Ulster is absolutely undiminished.

In the City of Dublin, in the City of Cork, in the City of Limerick, in almost every county in the South and West of Ireland, large, enthusiastic meetings, attended by thousands of Unionists, have been held denouncing the Home Rule Bill as being destructive to the best interests of our country, and affirming our determination to remain citizens of the British Empire.

Ten thousand pounds has been subscribed by the Unionists of the Southern and Western Provinces, within the last few months, in support of the campaign of the Irish Unionist Alliance against Home Rule. This sum has been mainly subscribed in small sums, as shown in the Dublin and Cork daily Press.

It is quite true that the Unionists are in a minority in these provinces, and consequently are not in a position to take up the same attitude as their brethren in Ulster, but their position should none the less attract the sympathy and assistance of the loyal population of Great Britain.

They represent substantial business interests; they contribute in many cases the largest share in the rates and taxes of their districts; they have been faithful to the Empire, and, viewing, as they do, with the greatest alarm this measure of Home Rule, and believing it means financial ruin and social disorder, and that it will bring about the disruption of the Empire, they demand that before the disastrous step is taken, they should have an opportunity of laying the true facts before the British people and taking their verdict at a General Election. Yours, etc.,

BARRYMORE

Chairman, Executive Committee.

Extract from an open letter from Baron Barrymore, chairman of the IUA
Published in the English press, 13 October 1913

Source 2

… Ulster looms very largely in this controversy, simply because Ulster has a strong right arm, but there are Unionists in the south and west who loath the bill just as much as we Ulster people loath it, whose difficulties are far greater, and who would willingly fight, as Ulster would fight, if they had the numbers. Nobody knows the difficulties of these men better than I do. Why, it was only the other day some of them ventured to put forward as a business proposition that this bill would be financial ruin to their businesses, saying no more, and immediately they were boycotted, and resolutions were passed, and they were told that they ought to understand as Protestants that they ought to be thankful and grateful for being allowed to live in peace among the people who are there. Yes, we can never support the bill which hands these people over to the tender mercies of those who have always been their bitterest enemies. We must go on whatever happens, opposing the bill to the end. That we are entitled to do; that we are bound to do. But I want to speak explicitly about the exclusion of Ulster … If the exclusion of Ulster is not shut out, and if at the same time the prime minister says he cannot admit anything contrary to the fundamental principles of the bill, I think it follows that the exclusion of Ulster is not contrary to the fundamental principles of the bill … On the other hand I say this, that your suggestions – no matter what paper safeguards you put, or no matter what other methods you may attempt to surround these safeguards with for the purpose of raising what I call 'your reasonable atmosphere' – if your suggestions try to compel these people to come into a Dublin parliament, I tell you I shall regardless of personal consequences, go on with these people to the end with their policy of resistance.

Extract from Sir Edward Carson's speech to House of Commons, 11 February 1914
HC Deb 5th series, vol 58

Source 3

*The Liberal government's inertia over Ulster – the Prime Minister,
H.H. Asquith's 'masterly inactivity' – had perhaps a more solid rationale
than some commentators have allowed. It was a strategy based not upon
ignorance or carelessness but upon intelligence reports of the condition of
Ulster Unionism. Simply by doing nothing, Asquith could permit the Unionist
leadership to become prisoners of their own logic, penned in by their own
indecision over violence, and by their own supporters' desire for a more
assertive command. Aggression, by any realistic assessment, threatened
sympathy in England; inertia threatened morale in Ireland, as was increasingly
clear within the UVF by late 1913. In so far as the Unionist leaders showed
themselves willing to negotiate with Liberals and Home Rulers, even in the
potentially most compromising of venues, in so far as they radically scaled
down their demands between 1911–12 and 1914, then Asquith's 'strategy' of
delay was rather more than an euphemism for indifference or idleness …*

*Asquith had not responded by substantial concession, and the Unionist
political leadership was therefore left in the talons of the hawks within the
Ulster Volunteer Force. The preliminary decision to fund a major gun-running
expedition was taken only in January 1914, in the context – significantly – of
the abortive private negotiations conducted between Carson, Bonar Law, and
Asquith. It represented a climbdown by the political leadership of Unionism,
and a recognition of the futility of the existing strategy. In this sense, the Larne
gun running, dazzling as a tactical coup, also reflected a profound strategic
failure for Carson and his political intimates.*

*Carson's increasingly apocalyptic rhetoric in the spring of 1914 … indicated
the quandary which he felt Unionism was in. Violence for Carson was certainly
an option – the last option – but he perceived violence in icily realistic
terms: as honourable, but also as suicidal. After Larne, when the penalties
of incitement were inescapable (because enthusiastic Unionists were now
armed), Carson softened his tone. It was as if Larne was an end in itself – as
if it alone had been sufficient to satisfy the military honour of the Ulster
Unionist movement, and the personal honour of its leaders.*

*The effective value of the gun running, beyond the undoubtedly central issues
of morale and publicity, is questionable. It consolidated the firepower of the
UVF, but then – given the Curragh 'Mutiny' – such an exercise was largely
redundant for the British were no longer in a position to impose a military*

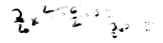

> settlement. Moreover, the UVF did not need Larne to be able to overwhelm the poorly organised and poorly equipped Irish Volunteer movement.
>
> **From Alvin Jackson, 'The Larne Gun Running of 1914'** (*History Ireland*, **Spring 1993**)

Q1

Consult Sources 1 and 2. Explain and compare the views of Barrymore and Carson on Southern Unionist and Ulster Unionist opposition to Home Rule for Ireland.

Baron Barrymore's open letter indicates that Southern Unionists were struggling to make an impact in the campaign against Home Rule by the autumn of 1913. This is a frank admission considering the money and energy expended by Southern Unionists in their propaganda blitz in Britain. In spite of these efforts, as the source demonstrates, their position was being "overlooked by the people of Great Britain". In analysing this failure Barrymore points to the huge publicity surrounding the preparations for armed resistance in Ulster, which have obviously "overshadowed" Southern Unionist efforts. Clearly, their lack of numbers in the three Southern provinces has closed the option of Southern Unionists following the Ulster lead on military preparations. Nevertheless, Barrymore is keen to emphasise that Southern Unionist opposition to Home Rule remains "undiminished". He describes the well attended, enthusiastic public meetings and the recent collection of £10,000 for the Irish Unionist Alliance's continuing propaganda campaign. The IUA, the principal Southern Unionist organisation in spite of its name, directed the propaganda campaign on the mainland and organised speakers for public meetings. Barrymore also makes a direct appeal for British help, as he seeks to benefit from the strong links and family ties that existed between Southern Unionists and British Conservatives. Southern Unionists put their faith in parliamentary opposition to Home Rule, and they continued to rely on their considerable influence in the House of Lords where they dominated Irish representation. While they acknowledge their lack of numbers, Southern Unionists stress their contribution to the Irish economy and society, an argument which undoubtedly carried some weight at the time. Although the Lords' veto had been removed in 1911, elections were still held on a restricted franchise, and Southern Unionists viewed themselves as the governing class. Not surprisingly, Barrymore closes with the staple Southern Unionist argument that Home Rule for Ireland would cause lasting damage to the British Empire.

While Barrymore's letter refers to Ulster Unionists as "brethren", it also contains a hint that Southern Unionists have some reservations about the strategy adopted by Ulster Unionists. This view is endorsed by Patrick Buckland who notes that Southern Unionists felt unable to support fully Ulster's armed preparations for resisting Home Rule, often complaining of what they described as *Carsonism*. It is possible to argue, therefore, that Southern Unionist support for Ulster exclusion from Home Rule was tactical, as they believed that a devolved parliament with Ulster excluded would be unacceptable to Nationalists who would, accordingly, withdraw their demand for Home Rule.

In Source 2, however, Carson does not hide his sympathy for the plight of Southern Unionists who were of course his own people. He stresses that Southern Unionists are just as determined to resist Home Rule as Ulster Unionists and, moreover, would undertake armed resistance if they had the numbers. This identification with his fellow Southern Unionists highlights the personal dilemma in which Carson found himself during the Home Rule crisis. From the outset he had devised a strategy of using Ulster resistance to smash the Third Home Rule Bill altogether, but it had already become clear that he would have to abandon this course of action and try to save as much of Ulster as he could from coming under a new Home Rule parliament in Dublin. Indeed, Carson had indicated as much back in September 1913, when he confided to Bonar Law that they should press for the exclusion of six Ulster counties. Up to that point Alvin Jackson has argued that Carson still hoped he could stop the bill but, thereafter, he became fatalistic. It seems that the publication of details for the establishment of an Ulster Provisional Government, which occurred in September 1913, finally forced Carson to accept reality. Of course, this meant a parting of the ways with the Southern Unionists, as Carson now concentrated on fighting for Ulster exclusion. Clearly, this was a difficult decision for Carson, because it would leave the Southern Unionists in an even more vulnerable situation, something which he alludes to in Source 2. In essence, Carson's speech is public confirmation that he has abandoned his fellow Unionists in the three Southern provinces. He is telling the House of Commons that Ulster Unionists intend to fight any attempt to force Home Rule on them, and his threat to "go on with these people to the end with their policy of resistance" is significant, as Carson was privy to Fred Crawford's gun running operation. While Carson, in the final instance, may have recoiled from actual violence against the forces of the Crown, he was certainly prepared to play a dangerous game of brinkmanship; this strategy was not, as Source 1 confirms, open to Southern Unionists. At the same time, in spite of such grave warnings, Carson's speech marks a compromise for the Unionist leadership which was pulling back from outright opposition to Home Rule for Ireland to focus on the exclusion of all or part of Ulster. In charting this

115

new course Carson states that "Ulster has a strong right arm", and in so doing highlights the Ulster Unionist emphasis on self-reliance; this contrasts sharply with Barrymore's appeal for help from the British public. Furthermore, the final demand in Source 1 for Home Rule to be put to the British public in a general election illustrates the Southern Unionist focus on a parliamentary strategy, whereas Carson's threat of armed resistance demonstrates Ulster Unionist readiness to pursue an extra-parliamentary, or unconstitutional course.

Q2

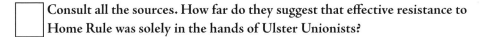

Consult all the sources. How far do they suggest that effective resistance to Home Rule was solely in the hands of Ulster Unionists?

Overall, the sources do suggest that Ulster Unionists were shouldering the main burden of opposition to Home Rule, but Source 3 also questions the effectiveness of the Ulster Unionist strategy.

In Source 1 Lord Barrymore, who was Chairman of the IUA, admits that Southern Unionists were making little impact in the anti-Home Rule campaign. They did not have the numbers to threaten armed resistance, and, as Barrymore acknowledges, their efforts were being overshadowed by the actions of the Ulstermen. Unlike their more parochial associates in the North, Southern Unionists were looking to Britain for sympathy and support, though their demand for a general election on the Home Rule issue, echoing Conservative calls, was contemptuously dismissed by the Liberal government. Barrymore claims that opposition to Home Rule in the three Southern provinces is "undiminished" and that their political rallies attract large numbers of enthusiastic supporters of the Union, but this was not having the desired effect on the mainland where the activities of the UVF were hogging the headlines. Source 1 also states the importance of the IUA's propaganda campaign in Southern Unionist strategy, the extent of which is noted by Buckland, but there is no assessment by Barrymore of its influence on opinion in Britain during the crisis of 1912–14.

Source 2 contains a grave warning from Carson that the government can expect that any attempt to impose Home Rule on Ulster will be met with armed resistance. The UVF, which was to receive a large consignment of weapons in April 1914, gave the Ulster Unionists "a strong right arm" which they intended to use. Historians such as Patricia Jalland have indicated that by this stage of the crisis the threats of violence made by the Ulster Unionist leadership and the prospect of civil war were taking their toll on the government's nerve, prompting senior figures in the Liberal Cabinet to consider possible concessions to the Ulstermen. Yet the source does not completely endorse the view that Ulster Unionist pressure was bearing fruit. In one sense Carson's speech is an admission of failure. His strategy of using Ulster resistance to block Home Rule for all of Ireland has been abandoned in favour of the more feasible objective of excluding Ulster from Home Rule. As David Miller has argued, Ulster Unionists would always vote against Home Rule for Ireland, but they were only prepared to fight for the exclusion of Ulster. Certainly, by February 1914 Carson realised that the Liberal government had no intention of withdrawing its Home Rule plans, and this pushed both sides towards the partition solution. Still, the Unionist leader was adamant that any attempt to coerce Ulster Unionists into a Home Rule parliament would result in violence. It is possible to argue, therefore, that Ulster Unionist opposition to Home Rule was effective, as it forced the government to renege on its commitment to the Irish Nationalists and look for a compromise.

In Source 3 the distinguished historian Alvin Jackson casts doubt on the impact of Ulster Unionist threats of violence. He suggests that the leadership's decision in January 1914 to sanction a major gun running operation was really a political disaster for Carson, who had been backed into a corner by Unionist extremists. Jackson describes Carson's fears about the consequences of using violence in the event of the Liberal government standing firm. While Carson may have regarded armed resistance as an option, he knew that it could prove disastrous for Ulster Unionists. In analysing the impact of the Larne gun running Jackson offers the opinion that it had little value in military terms, merely transforming the UVF from an unarmed force into a badly armed force. After the Curragh 'Mutiny' in March 1914, moreover, there was no point in arming the UVF, because the government dared not risk deploying the army in Ulster. In Jackson's view the real success of the Larne gun running lay in its propaganda effect and the boost to the morale of the rank and file. While the article deals exclusively with Ulster Unionist resistance to Home Rule, it argues that Unionist threats were not working as the government refused to bow to Unionist pressure. Indeed, it was noticeable that Carson moderated his stance after the gun running as he searched for a compromise solution to the Ulster impasse. For Jackson, therefore, there were obvious limits to the effectiveness of Ulster Unionist strategy. Actual violence would have cost the Ulstermen support on the mainland and imposed a serious strain on relations with their Southern Unionist brethren, while violent rhetoric was having a negligible effect on the Liberal government. This leads Jackson to conclude that the real purpose of the Larne gun running was to mollify extremists, such as Fred Crawford, who were impatient with the Unionist leadership's lack of direct action.

Q3

Consult all the sources. Which of them would a historian value most in a study of the nature of Ulster Unionist resistance to Home Rule?

All of the sources are useful in assessing the nature of Ulster Unionist resistance to Home Rule in 1913–14.

While the focus in Source 1 is on the actions of Southern Unionists in the anti-Home Rule struggle, there are important references to the impact of Ulster Unionist plans for armed resistance. Barrymore concludes that the Ulster Unionist strategy is dominating all opposition to Home Rule, completely overshadowing the sterling efforts being made by supporters of the Union in the South. By the autumn of 1913 there was little evidence of concerted *Irish* Unionist opposition to Home Rule, as the separate organisations sought to build on their strengths. The formation of the Ulster Unionist Council in 1905 had presented Ulster Unionists with the means to develop a separate strategy, and the concentration of numbers in the North East allowed them to engage in direct action with the formation of the UVF. It is Barrymore's view that the threat of armed resistance has seized the public's attention in the rest of the United Kingdom. Of course, Barrymore's letter is very tactful, and it did make an impact in Britain, a view which Lord Lansdowne, the Conservative leader in the House of Lords and himself a Southern Unionist, subsequently expressed to Carson. As Buckland has argued, Southern Unionists exerted considerable influence in Britain at the time, principally through their contacts with the Conservative Party. Ulster Unionists, by contrast, never enjoyed this level of cooperation with the Conservatives, though Carson and Bonar Law enjoyed a very close working relationship. As Chairman of the IUA, Barrymore was obviously a high-ranking Southern Unionist, and his letter can also be regarded as a subtle reminder to both Carson and the Conservative Party that a storm of protest would follow any move to abandon them. Barrymore is clearly concerned that, in Jackson's phrase, Ulster Unionists might become "prisoners of their own logic", as their strategy of outright opposition to Home Rule switched to a compromise on the basis of Ulster exclusion. Therefore, Source 1 is of value because it hints at Southern Unionist fears that they will be abandoned, as Ulster Unionists seek to save themselves from Home Rule.

Source 2 is a useful document, as it captures the public face of the Ulster Unionist leadership in the early part of 1914. Carson had already sanctioned the gun running in January, and his assertion that Ulster has "a strong right arm" is, on the surface, a powerful indication that Ulster Unionists will resort to violence if any attempt is made to place them under a Home Rule parliament. This illustrates both the determined nature of Ulster Unionist resistance and the leader's personal commitment to the Ulster Unionist cause. Carson was perhaps the leading lawyer practising in London at the time, but he was apparently prepared to risk his life and liberty in pursuit of the Ulster Unionist cause. While Carson was prepared to indulge in militant rhetoric, however, he was much more moderate behind the scenes, engaging in a series of private talks in an attempt to find a political solution. Although his speech in the House of Commons is a reminder of his identification with the Southern Unionists, it is clear that Carson is now fighting for the exclusion of Ulster from Home Rule and totally rejecting what he regarded as inadequate assurances for Unionists. Source 2 is particularly useful for understanding the shift in Unionist strategy which took place against a backdrop of uncompromising rhetoric – rhetoric which could not hide Carson's change of direction. He is now reluctantly abandoning his fellow Southern Unionists, accepting that Home Rule will apply to the three Southern provinces.

Source 3 offers the view of a well-informed historian who argues that Carson was by no means as confident as his public speeches indicated. In focusing on the UVF spectacular at Larne, moreover, Jackson claims that the gun running was primarily a propaganda exercise to appease the Unionist hawks. Although Carson had taken an increasingly militant stance in his opposition to Home Rule during the course of 1913, the Liberal government had refused to buckle. In fact, Asquith had stuck closely to his policy of refusing to consider any concessions to his opponents until the Home Rule Bill was on its final parliamentary circuit, a tactic criticised by a number of historians who claimed that it deepened the crisis. However, Jackson takes issue with this contention, claiming that Asquith's "masterly inactivity" actually forced the Unionist leadership to take a more responsible approach as they came to appreciate the consequences of armed resistance. Patricia Jalland has taken the opposite view, arguing that Asquith missed an opportunity to seize the initiative in 1912 by following up the Agar Robartes' proposal, but there is much to commend the Jackson thesis that such a move would only have fuelled Unionist demands for further concessions. Source 3 explains that the Liberal government's Home Rule strategy was informed by regular intelligence briefings from Ulster, which must have thrown some light on Carson's nervousness about the use of violence, and Jackson's description of armed resistance "as honourable, but also as suicidal" is very convincing. He also demonstrates that the Larne episode really made Carson's search for a compromise more urgent as the situation in Ulster was now much more explosive. After the gun running the Unionist leadership ran the risk of a serious outbreak of violence which could only damage the Unionist cause on the mainland. Source 3 makes reference to the failure of the private talks between Carson, Bonar Law and Asquith, which may have prompted the gun running but exposed the political weakness of the Ulster Unionist position. Carson's actions after the

119

gun running, when he redoubled his efforts to find a compromise solution based on exclusion, confirm the accuracy of Jackson's analysis. Therefore, while both Sources 1 and 2 shed valuable light on the nature of Ulster Unionist resistance to Home Rule in the 1913–14 period, Source 3 goes further; it looks behind the public face of Ulster Unionist resistance and analyses the complex problems facing the Unionist leadership as it struggled to control its more militant followers while threatening the Liberal government with armed resistance.

Nationalists and Home Rule

Source 1

*As the crisis deepened, in February 1914 the Unionist leader,
Sir Edward Carson – worried perhaps by the militancy of his supporters in
the Ulster Volunteers – made a statesmanlike speech calling for his 'nationalist
fellow countrymen' to try to win over the Ulster Unionists by sympathetic
understanding rather than political manoeuvre. The speech affected
Redmond deeply; he started to talk of a compromise based on county option,
whereby counties with a Unionist majority could opt out of the Home Rule
scheme – but only on a temporary six-year basis. It took an effort to go even
this far: Joe Devlin in particular was doing everything to hold Redmond to an
Irish unity position. Nevertheless, Redmond's close aide, Stephen Gwynn, felt
that the Irish leader had not gone quite far enough in pursuit of reconciliation.*

**From Paul Bew, *John Redmond*, Historical Association of Ireland
(Dundalgan Press, 1996)**

Source 2

*We do not believe the reality of the threats of civil war indulged in by
Sir Edward Carson and his followers. We have exceptional sources of
information in regard to the Ulster Volunteer movement, and we are convinced
that its danger is grossly exaggerated. The main ground for this conviction is
the fact that in Belfast, the headquarters of the Carsonite movement, where
the Catholic and Protestant home rulers would be amongst the first victims of
any outbreak among the Orangemen, the home rulers regard the whole thing
with absolute contempt, and are astonished that anybody outside Belfast
should take it seriously …*

*We believe the case could be met by permitting 'Ulster' to claim exclusion
after, say, ten years if her representatives were not satisfied with their
treatment in the Irish Parliament … The record of Catholic and Nationalist
Ireland, now and always, is proof of its toleration … The inclusion of 'Ulster'
with the right of going out after a trial period, affords the best means of
practically testing its reliability …*

… We would be in favour of giving 'Ulster' extra representation in the Irish

---

Parliament ... [and] ... such an arrangement of the Senate as would afford them an additional safeguard ...

**Extract from a memo from Joe Devlin to Lloyd George,
20 February 1914
NLI: John Redmond Papers, MS 15181 (3)**

Source 3

I would therefore suggest that any county in Ireland that wished to submit its case once more to the British electorate for decision should be allowed to contract out of the Act. The opinion of the counties would be taken by means of a plebiscite of the electors in each county ... If the poll should be in favour of exclusion, that particular county would be excluded from the operation of the Act for X years ...

During the period of temporary exclusion, these counties would be governed by and represented in the Imperial Parliament in the same way exactly as at the present moment ... With the exception of these four counties, the whole of Ireland would come immediately under the operation of the Home Rule Bill. It would be almost impossible for them to justify armed resistance in these counties at the present moment if such an option were given them; and the same observation applies even if they rejected it.

Extract from a letter from Lloyd George to Cabinet, February 1914

Q1

Consult Sources 1 and 2. Explain and compare the views of Redmond and Devlin in their attitude to the Unionist position in early 1914.

In Source 1 the distinguished historian Paul Bew argues that Redmond made a serious attempt to empathise with Unionist difficulties in February 1914. Redmond had been moved by an appeal by the Unionist leader, Sir Edward Carson, who called on his "nationalist fellow countrymen" to win over Ulster Unionists to the idea of Home Rule by argument and understanding. Clearly, Redmond felt under pressure to respond to Carson's appeal in a statesman-like manner, demonstrating that he was flexible and willing to compromise. A willingness to consider "county option" was, of course, a significant climbdown for the IPP leader; he had been unequivocal in his celebrated Limerick speech on 12 October 1913, when he warned that Irish Nationalists could never agree to the mutilation of the Irish nation. By February 1914, however, it is clear that he was giving serious consideration to a compromise based on allowing the counties with a Unionist majority to be excluded from the Home Rule scheme for six years. Effectively, this meant that the four plantation counties, Antrim, Down, Londonderry and Armagh – those with Unionist/Protestant majorities – would opt out of the operation of the Home Rule arrangements for a six-year period. This change in Redmond's thinking came in spite of pressure from Joe Devlin, the leading Ulster Nationalist, who insisted that Redmond must not abandon the one nation position he had articulated in Limerick. Up until this point Redmond relied on Asquith's Liberal government to resist Unionist pressure and deliver Home Rule on an all-Ireland basis. In his contact with the government he reiterated the Devlin line that threats of Unionist resistance and possible civil war were scaremongering tactics that should be ignored. Yet throughout 1913 Carson had clearly raised the stakes, indulging in violent rhetoric and apparently conniving with the hawks in Ulster who were engaged in military preparations. There is a suggestion in Source 1, however, that Carson was moderating his stance in the early part of 1914, and Redmond was responding to this move. The two leaders probably had a mutual respect for each other, a respect that could have developed from their earlier association on the Leinster legal circuit. By February 1914 the Home Rule struggle had reached a dangerous stalemate, and Redmond was anxious to break that stalemate. While he was not prepared to go to the lengths advocated by Stephen Gwynn, his close colleague and confidant, Redmond was nevertheless willing to offer a concession in order to break the stalemate and help the Liberal government resolve the present impasse. In making this move the Irish leader was also responding to Unionist fears, and he clearly hoped that his magnanimous gesture would be followed by a reasonable Unionist response following the six-year exclusion period. Therefore, while Redmond had previously dismissed dire warnings from Ulster as wild exaggeration, by February 1914 he was attempting to show Unionists in Ulster that Nationalists were prepared to respond to their fears.

Source 2 reveals that Devlin has taken a different view of Unionist threats and difficulties. Devlin, the MP for West Belfast, had consistently argued that Carson and his followers were engaged in a game of bluff. The formation of the Ulster Volunteers and the subsequent military preparations had not altered Devlin's views, and he claims to have "exceptional sources of information" on the UVF to support his position. From his Belfast vantage point Devlin dismisses the danger posed by Unionists as "grossly exaggerated". In particular, he notes that the Catholic population of Belfast, who would be the first victims of Unionist violence, are remarkably sanguine about their security. If Belfast Nationalists are unconcerned with Unionist threats, Devlin argues, then Nationalists in the rest of Ireland should dismiss warnings of serious unrest. Yet the fact that Devlin is also prepared to consider some form of compromise, albeit one that does not go as far as Redmond's, is an indication of the pressure being applied by the government in early 1914. Behind the scenes the Liberal government was considering various schemes, all designed to placate Ulster Unionist opposition to the Third Home Rule Bill. Devlin's suggestion is to offer "Ulster", although this is not defined, the opportunity to withdraw from the Home Rule parliament after a set period if her representatives are dissatisfied with their treatment by the administration in Dublin. Of course, Devlin's memorandum reveals his confidence in the performance of an Irish parliament, which would behave impartially during the trial period and, therefore, remove the demand for Ulster exclusion. And Devlin was prepared to go further, as Source 2 outlines plans for providing Unionists with additional seats in a proposed Upper House (senate) in order to balance the expected Nationalist majority in the Lower House.

Therefore, while both men were sceptical about the Unionist threat of serious violence, and in this Redmond was dependent on advice from Devlin – the eyewitness observer in Belfast – Redmond was more conciliatory and was prepared to abandon the unity position, if only for a temporary period. Devlin, on the other hand, insisted that the Home Rule Bill should proceed on an all-Ireland basis, though he was prepared to concede some form of exclusion after ten years, confident that the performance of the Home Rule parliament in Dublin would render such a step unnecessary.

Q2

Consult all the sources. How far do they suggest that the county option scheme was a viable proposal in early February 1914?

Overall, the sources do suggest that a county option scheme might have been a workable compromise, but Source 2 outlines the Ulster Nationalist opposition to any tampering with the Union and there is no indication of Unionist attitudes to such a proposal.

Source 1 suggests that the search for a solution to the Ulster impasse had now become more urgent. Carson was clearly worried by the growing militancy of his followers, and his appeal for Nationalist understanding of the Unionist position had drawn a positive response from Redmond. At the time, of course, the IPP leader was coming under increasing pressure from the Liberal government to make some kind of compromise gesture, and he had known from his private meetings with leading Cabinet figures in November 1913 that the government was giving serious consideration to some kind of county option scheme. By February 1914 Redmond was prepared, in spite of pressure from Devlin, to make such an offer in order to secure agreement on Home Rule. This was a major departure from the position that he had outlined in his Limerick speech, but Source 1 states that he was now willing to break what the historian Robert Kee has described as the one-Ireland principle. Clearly, Redmond believed that such a generous offer by Nationalists would be sufficient to avert possible Unionist violence and allow Home Rule to be implemented. For his part, Carson probably assumed that he had made a significant compromise by abandoning the three Southern provinces and continuing the struggle on the basis of securing the exclusion of all or part of Ulster. Still, there is nothing in Source 1 to suggest that Ulster Unionists considered county option to be a viable proposal. In all likelihood this would not have been enough for Unionists, as Carson's contemptuous dismissal of the county option scheme indicated when the issue came before parliament in March 1914. Source 1 also highlights the fact that Redmond viewed county option as a temporary measure, insisting that Home Rule would be implemented on an all-Ireland basis at the end of the exclusion period. While some of his colleagues, such as Stephen Gwynn, urged Redmond to drop any time limit on exclusion, Redmond knew that he would have to persuade Devlin and his Ulster followers to endorse his proposal, meaning exclusion had to be on a temporary basis.

Source 2 reveals that Devlin is sticking to the unity principle, but that even he, in spite of his dismissal of Unionist warnings, is prepared to consider some kind of compromise. Devlin's assessment of the situation in February 1914 indicates that he does not consider county option necessary. This is because, in his opinion, if the Liberal government proceeds with the Home Rule Bill in its original form, Unionist threats of civil strife will prove to be wild exaggerations. As a representative of a Belfast constituency, Devlin of course knew that implementation of the county option scheme would mean the exclusion of the four plantation counties – Antrim, Down, Londonderry and Armagh – and that East Ulster Nationalists would be at the mercy of their Unionist opponents. For Devlin, therefore, county option was not a viable answer in February 1914. However, his willingness to consider alternative solutions to meet Unionist objections suggests that he might be persuaded to endorse county option if it is deemed necessary to establish Home Rule for the remaining 28 counties. It is also true that leading Liberals were confident that Devlin would, in spite of his repeated articulation of the unity principle, fall into line with the IPP leadership. Therefore, while Source 2 suggests that, on the surface, Devlin does not regard county option as a viable alternative, there is some inkling from his readiness to consider other solutions that the leading Ulster Nationalist might be persuaded to support some type of county option scheme – on the clear understanding that it would be temporary.

Source 3 confirms that Lloyd George who by this stage was the dominant figure in the Cabinet on the Home Rule issue, views county option as a workable strategy. In June 1912 the backbench Liberal MP, Thomas Agar-Robartes, moved an amendment to the Home Rule Bill, proposing that the four plantation counties be excluded from the operation of the bill. This presented the Liberal government with the opportunity to seize the initiative and throw the Unionists into confusion, but the historian Patricia Jalland argues that Asquith failed to see the potential for an early settlement based on some form of Ulster exclusion. Yet by February 1914 the Cabinet did consider such a move as a viable solution to the Ulster crisis. In the last sentence of the memorandum Lloyd George justifies the government's new stance by emphasising that the offer of county option will make it impossible for Ulster Unionists to contemplate armed resistance, whether they support or reject it. It was, therefore, an appropriate solution for the government, because Lloyd George persuaded his colleagues that it would be viewed in Britain as a reasonable offer, the rejection of which would alienate public opinion on the mainland. In these circumstances he was certain that Unionists would recoil from violence. Source 3 also stresses the temporary nature of the county option scheme, as the government recognised that this was essential if Nationalist backing was to be secured, though the actual time period is unspecified. It is also clear that the government was responding to Unionist resistance, and this fell into line with Asquith's Home Rule strategy. While the Liberals insisted through 1912–13 that Home Rule would be implemented on an all-Ireland basis, Asquith had informed his Cabinet colleagues that some type of concession on Ulster might well be necessary, but he would delay making it for as long as possible.

In conclusion, Sources 1 and 3 make it clear that the county option proposal was a viable solution to the Ulster impasse, but there is nothing to indicate Unionist reaction to such an offer. In June 1912 the Agar-Robartes' amendment had initially thrown the Unionists into confusion, but they subsequently agreed to support it as a wrecking amendment. Source 2 suggests that Devlin and the Ulster Nationalists will oppose any proposal that compromised the unity principle, but Devlin is willing to consider alternative proposals that might alleviate Unionist fears.

Q3

Consult all the sources. Which would a historian value most in a study of attempts to find a solution to the Ulster problem in 1914?

All of the sources would be useful to a historian studying attempts to solve the Ulster problem in 1914. Source 1, an extract from Paul Bew's brief biography of Redmond, sheds valuable light on the Irish leader's motives in considering the county option compromise. Redmond had been moved by Carson's "statesman-like speech" pleading with Nationalists to convert Ulster Unionists to the idea of Home Rule through argument and "understanding". This was a challenge that Redmond could not refuse. Source 1 also emphasises Devlin's opposition to any concession on the one-Ireland principle and illustrates his efforts to hold Redmond to "an Irish unity position". Of course, in the end Devlin was prepared to sacrifice Irish unity, as Redmond probably anticipated, for the sake of party unity and he subsequently backed the proposals on the basis that it would be temporary. Yet Source 1 indicates that there was a train of thought within the IPP which suggested that Redmond should embrace an even greater compromise and drop the time limit altogether. While Redmond was not willing to go this far, Source 1, and Devlin's willingness to consider some other method of appeasing Unionist opposition, demonstrate that Nationalists were engaged in a genuine attempt to find a solution to the Ulster impasse. What Source 1 does not convey is the pressure Redmond was under from the Liberal government to agree to a compromise on Ulster. Therefore, Redmond was responding to both government pressure and to the emotional appeal made by Carson referred to in Source 1. The Bew extract is also very useful because it hints at the dilemma now facing Carson, who was increasingly worried by "the militancy of his supporters". As the historian Alvin Jackson has noted, Carson had by this stage become the "prisoner" of Ulster Unionism, and he was anxious to direct his followers towards compromise and away from violence. Therefore, Source 1 suggests a willingness by both Carson and Redmond to work towards a political compromise in the early part of 1914.

Source 2 demonstrates that there were significant obstacles in the way of such a compromise. The Belfast Nationalist leader, Joe Devlin, could not accept that Ulster Unionists would engage in serious violence if the Home Rule Bill proceeded in its current form. Devlin's claim to be "astonished" that anyone outside Belfast should give serious consideration to such threats is evidence of the reassurance that Redmond was receiving from his supporters in Ulster. While this illustrates the difficulty in finding a workable solution to the Ulster problem, Devlin's alternative proposals to placate Ulster Unionists indicate that there was a growing readiness on the Nationalist side to make significant concessions. This makes Source 2 a useful document. That Nationalists faced such difficulties in the early part of 1914 was one consequence of Redmond's failure to realise the seriousness of the situation in 1913. As Robert Kee has argued, he had become too dependent on Liberal goodwill and had no contingency plan once the government opted for compromise. The real benefit of Source 2 is, therefore, that it shows Devlin, who was one of the IPP's strongest opponents of special treatment for Ulster, willing to support the inclusion of a number of safeguards for Unionists in an attempt to solve the Ulster problem.

Source 3, the Cabinet memorandum tabled by the leading government minister Lloyd George, is a valuable document as it confirms his intention to support the addition of a county option scheme. Lloyd George had played the key role in the government's search for a solution to the Ulster problem, and this document states his preference for county option over the alternative of Home Rule within Home Rule, which he had now rejected. For Nationalists to swallow such a bitter pill there is a clear statement that it will be temporary. In fact, the final proposal accepted by Redmond at the beginning of March 1914 specified a six-year time limit, though this of course would mean a general election in the intervening period. Source 3 also reveals Lloyd George's intention to undermine the Unionist position, as he is confident that Ulster Unionists cannot justify armed resistance in the four excluded counties if they are offered such a reasonable concession. Indeed, Lloyd George seeks to reassure his Cabinet colleagues that this is a 'win-win' situation for the government, because even if Unionists reject the county option proposals they will no longer be in a position to justify armed resistance. After such a prolonged period of political deadlock Lloyd George was convinced that he had produced a compromise which would provide the basis for a working arrangement for both Unionists and Nationalists. Although the proposals outlined in Source 3 were subsequently rejected by Carson, it provides a clear view of the government's thinking in 1914. It was clear that Nationalists would be pressed to make the decisive move and break the one-Ireland principle.

While Sources 2 and 3 offer valuable insights into both the Liberal government's and Nationalist thinking on the Ulster problem in February 1914, Source 1 is the most useful. It is wider in scope, suggesting Carson's desire for a settlement and outlining the thinking behind Redmond's change of heart on the unity principle. It was this concession which offered some prospect of a successful resolution of the Ulster problem in 1914.

THE CAUSES OF THE RISING

Source 1

I have come to the conclusion that the Gaelic League, as the Gaelic League, is a spent force; and I am glad of it … Our Gaelic League time was to be our tutelage: we had first to learn to know Ireland, to read the lineaments of her face, to understand the accents of her voice; to repossess ourselves, disinherited as we were, of her spirit and mind, re-enter into our mystical birthright … To every generation its deed. The deed of the generation that has now reached middle life was the Gaelic League: the beginning of the Irish Revolution. Let our generation not shirk its deed, which is to accomplish the revolution … I am glad, then, that the North has 'begun'. I am glad that the Orangemen have armed, for it is a goodly thing to see arms in Irish hands. I should like to see the AOH armed. I should like to see the Transport Workers armed. I should like to see any and every body of Irish citizens armed. We must accustom ourselves to the thought of arms, to the sight of arms, to the use of arms. We may make mistakes in the beginning and shoot the wrong people; but bloodshed is a cleansing and a sanctifying thing, and the nation which regards it as the final horror has lost its manhood. There are many things more horrible than bloodshed; and slavery is one of them.

Extract from Patrick Pearse, 'The Coming Revolution', November 1913
PH Pearse, *Political Writings and Speeches* (Phoenix, 1924)
(Originally published in the Gaelic League journal)

Source 2

This is a place of peace, sacred to the dead, where men should speak with all charity and with all restraint; but I hold it a Christian thing, as O'Donovan Rossa held it, to hate evil, to hate untruth, to hate oppression, and, hating them, to strive to overthrow them. Our foes are strong and wise and wary; but, strong and wise and wary as they are, they cannot undo the miracles of God who ripens in the hearts of young men the seeds sown by the young men of a former generation. And the seeds sown by the young men of '65 and '67 are coming to their miraculous ripening to-day. Rulers and Defenders of Realms had need to be wary if they would guard against such processes. Life springs from death; and from the graves of patriot men and women spring living nations. The Defenders of this Realm have worked well in secret and in the open. They think that they have pacified Ireland. They think that they have purchased half of us and intimidated the other half. They think that they have foreseen everything, think that they have provided against everything; but the fools, the fools, the fools! – they have left us our Fenian dead, and while Ireland holds these graves, Ireland unfree shall never be at peace.

Extract from Patrick Pearse's speech at the burial of O'Donovan Rossa, 1 August 1915
Ruth Dudley Edwards, *Patrick Pearse: The Triumph of Failure* (Poolbeg Press, 1990)

Source 3

Poblacht na h-Éireann

The Provisional Government of the Irish Republic to the People of Ireland

Irishmen and Irishwomen: In the name of God and of the dead generations from which she receives her old tradition of nationhood, Ireland, through us, summons her children to her flag and strikes for her freedom.

Having organised and trained her manhood through her secret revolutionary organisation, the Irish Republican Brotherhood, and through her open military organisations, the Irish Volunteers, and the Irish Citizen Army, having patiently perfected her discipline, having resolutely waited for the right moment to reveal itself, she now seizes that moment, and, supported by her exiled children in America and by gallant allies in Europe, but relying in the first on her own strength, she strikes in full confidence of victory ...

Signed on behalf of the provisional government,
THOMAS J CLARKE, SEAN MACDIARMADA, THOMAS MACDONAGH,
P H PEARSE, EAMONN CEANNT, JAMES CONNOLLY, JOSEPH PLUNKETT.

Extract, published in the English press, 1 May 1916

Q1

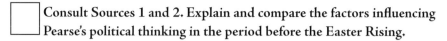

Consult Sources 1 and 2. Explain and compare the factors influencing Pearse's political thinking in the period before the Easter Rising.

In Source 1 Pearse is developing the ideas presented in Eoin MacNeill's article, 'The North Began', which appeared in the previous week's edition of the Gaelic League journal. MacNeill's article led directly to the formation of the Irish Volunteers at the end of November 1913, a development in which Pearse was to play a prominent role. Although he had earlier been a supporter of Redmond, by November 1913 Pearse was giving vent to a much more militant form of Nationalism. Pearse had been stirred by the actions of the Ulster Volunteers who had, in his opinion, pointed the way forward for Nationalists. Indeed, in 'The Coming Revolution' Pearse advocates the widespread dispersal of arms among Irish citizens, describing it as "a goodly thing to see arms in Irish hands". By this stage Pearse was turning away from the constitutional methods of Redmondism, arguing that violence, or at least the threat of violence, would be necessary for the achievement of nationhood. In fact, the glorification of violence is particularly striking in Source 1, and Pearse indulges in what one biographer has described as a "rhetoric of blood", when he claims that "bloodshed is a cleansing and a sanctifying thing". Clearly, Pearse is taking this opportunity to articulate the change in his political thinking. He had recently become a prominent political figure, and his article highlights his belief that the onus is on Pearse's generation to free Ireland from British rule. For Pearse, failure to use force will mean continued subjugation to England with Irish citizens condemned to "slavery". The change in Pearse's political thinking at this point is captured at the beginning of the article. He had been a leading figure in the Gaelic League, and it was the League that had, in Pearse's words, provided his "tutelage" by demonstrating what was meant by Irishness. Yet Pearse is now stating his belief that the League has served its purpose, and it is the task of his generation, having received its political education in the movement, to engage in a revolution aimed at winning Irish freedom. Therefore, the main factors influencing Pearse's political thinking in November 1913 were the impact of the UVF in Ulster, the growing realisation that his generation had a duty to strike for Irish freedom now that the Gaelic League had prepared the ground, and a new appreciation of the glory of bloodshed in the pursuit of nationhood.

Source 2 illustrates the consistency in his political thinking. Pearse is still talking about the responsibility of his generation, and there is a clear implication that a future insurrection is inevitable. Of course, the occasion of O'Donovan Rossa's funeral in August 1915 allowed Pearse to rouse his audience with fiery rhetoric. It was his greatest test as an orator, and he rose to the occasion by using a carefully crafted script which achieved precisely the reaction that the funeral organisers had intended. Jeremiah O'Donovan Rossa had been an old Fenian activist, and his funeral gave the Fenian, or IRB, leadership, the opportunity to stage a major propaganda event. Pearse had not joined the IRB until December 1913, several weeks after the publication of Source 1, and there is clear evidence of IRB influence in the famous grave-side oration. Pearse makes no reference to Unionist resistance to Home Rule or to the earlier work of the Gaelic League, instead concentrating on the importance of striking a blow for Irish freedom. In this Pearse stresses the tradition of revolutionary Nationalism in Ireland and includes a specific reference to the Fenian rebellion in the 1860s. Source 2 also warns of imminent revolution, something which had become more likely against the background of war in Europe, as the IRB sought to take advantage of England's difficulty. In spite of English skill and cunning, which has enabled them to control Ireland as they "purchased half of us and intimidated the other half", Pearse argues that his generation are ready to launch a rebellion. For inspiration he looks to the "graves of patriot men and women" which will spawn "living nations". Moreover, the war was beginning to influence Pearse, as it strengthened his commitment to the notion of a blood sacrifice. Here, the importance of martyrs and the references to the sacrifices of previous generations are emphasised. A final factor influencing Pearse's political thinking, which can be gleaned from Source 2, is his development as a romantic revolutionary figure. Pearse was not typical of leading IRB conspirators such as Tom Clarke, and his grave-side speech suggests that revolutionary Nationalism is morally correct and is, moreover, a pure, almost innocent, ideology.

While the obvious influence of Pearse's role in the IRB is evident in Source 2, there is a clear line of consistency in his thinking with his concentration on the need for violence to establish Irish freedom.

Q2

> **Consult all the sources. How does Pearse justify the use of violence to achieve freedom?**

Pearse advocates and justifies the use of violence to achieve freedom for Ireland in each of the sources. In Source 1 he states that it has fallen to his generation to carry the Irish revolution through to its conclusion, and this is a responsibility that must not be shirked. Pearse argues that Ireland can only attain her freedom through the use of violence, as without such a threat the Irish will only receive as much freedom as England is prepared to grant. By November 1913 Pearse, who had been a Redmond supporter, was convinced that Unionist pressure would see the Liberal government at Westminster renege on its commitment to Home Rule, and this was to prove a crucial factor in his conversion to revolutionary Nationalism. If Carson and the UVF could force concessions from the British government by the use of force, then Pearse thought it logical for Nationalists to follow the Unionist example. His article also suggests that violence by itself is necessary for a nation to assert its "manhood". Indeed, in his claim that bloodshed is "a cleansing and a sanctifying thing", Pearse goes further than his view that arms are a symbol of a nation's virility by suggesting that violence and bloodshed will be necessary to save Ireland's soul. Even the prospect of innocent lives being lost should not, in Pearse's opinion, prevent an armed insurrection, because the alternative is continued "slavery" for the Irish people.

In Source 2 Pearse uses his grave-side oration to articulate the IRB's commitment to overthrow oppression and the view that this could only be achieved through violence. At this point, Pearse introduces a new concept with his claim that God has brought Pearse's generation to the point of readiness for revolution, as God has ripened "the seeds sown by the young men of a former generation". Pearse concentrates on the tradition of violent Nationalism, which was in his view morally justified, and asserts that it is the responsibility of the youth of Ireland to maintain this tradition. Furthermore, the method of English rule, which has relied on a mixture of bribery and intimidation to keep Ireland under control, makes it reasonable for the Irish to use violence in order to end English occupation. Pearse closes his grave-side speech with another reference to the tradition of violent Nationalism in Ireland and to the cult of martyrdom – a feature of revolutionary Nationalism which, he argues, must be continued. In his reference to "our Fenian dead" Pearse justifies the use of future violence with the suggestion that his and succeeding generations have an obligation to Irish martyrs to continue the struggle for Irish freedom until success has been achieved. Finally, in his use of the memorable phrase "Life springs from death", there is a powerful religious undertone suggesting that death for such a glorious cause would rekindle the spirit of Irish nationality in the way that Christ had sacrificed himself to save mankind.

Source 3 is an extract from the proclamation of the Irish Republic, which was largely Pearse's work, and contains both an appeal for support from the Irish people and a justification for the actions of the insurgents. As in Source 2, God's name is invoked, and the choice of Easter for the Rising adds weight to the view that Pearse saw himself as a Messiah-like figure willing to sacrifice himself to save Ireland's soul. He is also launching the rebellion in the name of the "dead generations" which, he claims, have kept alive the spirit of nationhood by their attempts to establish a free Ireland through force of arms. Now it is the turn of Pearse's generation to maintain this tradition of violent Nationalism. The work done by his coconspirators in the IRB is acknowledged, and Pearse makes reference to his fellow insurgents in the

133

ranks of the Irish Volunteers and the Irish Citizen Army. Indeed, a key objective of his earlier speech at the O'Donovan Rossa funeral had been to establish a bond between the IRB, the Volunteers and the Citizen Army. In striking for Irish freedom Pearse states that these groups have been preparing for the insurrection and have waited patiently for the right moment. Of course, the insurgents felt their best prospect of a successful rebellion was when Britain was preoccupied with the war. The timing of the rebellion has been carefully planned, and Pearse enthusiastically urges his followers to seize "that moment", as a successful outcome is anticipated. On one level, therefore, Pearse is justifying violence by associating the Rising with the tradition of revolutionary Nationalism, and on another level he appears to justify the rebellion on the basis that it will achieve freedom. He mentions German assistance – their "gallant allies in Europe" – as increasing the likelihood of victory, but surely Pearse could not have been confident of victory. The arrest of Casement on Good Friday had thrown the Rising plans into confusion, and the interception of the German ship bringing 20,000 rifles for the Volunteers dashed the remote chance of victory that had existed. Nevertheless, Pearse and the Military Council of the IRB were determined to proceed, if only to keep alive the tradition of violent Nationalism.

To conclude, in each of the sources Pearse deploys a variety of arguments to justify the use of violence, but the most significant reason is his belief that Ireland can only achieve her freedom through violence and bloodshed.

Q3

Consult all the sources. Which would a historian value most in a study of the causes of the Easter Rising?

All of the sources shed light on the causes of the Rising, and each focuses on the crucial role played by Pearse – a key figure in the planning of the rebellion.

Source 1 is a very valuable document, as it charts Pearse's transition from a supporter of constitutional Nationalism to a revolutionary activist. Although Pearse had yet to join the IRB, his article in the Gaelic League journal suggests that IRB membership will be a logical progression. As early as November 1913, Pearse is advocating the use of violence as the only way to achieve freedom for Ireland, and there is a determination to break free from the present condition of "slavery". Source 1 makes a clear reference to the role played by the Gaelic League in the run-up to the Rising. This endorses FX Martin's argument that the League created the "atmosphere" for a rising, and FSL Lyons has emphasised that most of the men who turned towards violent Nationalism at this stage had "begun their apprenticeship inside the Gaelic League".

Indeed, in the years immediately before the Rising the IRB was recruiting heavily among Gaelic League enthusiasts just like Pearse. Pearse argues that the League has achieved its purpose by preparing the ground for a rebellion, and he continues by stating specifically that it is now the task of his generation to "accomplish the revolution". This is a very significant statement, coming as it did in November 1913. Although such rhetoric was a common feature of contemporary political writing, it marks the beginning of Pearse's realisation that only an armed insurrection could achieve freedom for Ireland, and he stuck closely to this view for the rest of his life. In addition, his article offers an indication of the development of his belief in blood sacrifice, and this was a key motivation for many of the 1916 leaders. Source 1 also touches on the impact of Carsonism and the UVF on revolutionary Nationalism, with its mention of arms in the hands of "Orangemen". Some historians, notably Michael Laffan, have argued that Carson "rekindled the Fenian flame", and Source 1 confirms Pearse's awareness of the unintended role played by the Unionist leader.

Source 2 gives some indication of IRB thinking one year after the outbreak of the war. It contains a clear commitment to a future insurrection amidst the high rhetoric of a carefully crafted piece of oratory. Pearse draws inspiration from the past heroes of revolutionary Nationalism who gave their lives in the cause of Ireland, and he shows that his generation is under an obligation to continue the sequence of armed rebellions. This demonstrates the significance of the tradition of revolutionary Nationalism for many of the 1916 leaders, particularly Pearse. Yet, while there is obvious IRB influence on Pearse's thinking, there is no inkling of the conspiracy to stage a rebellion which was already in place. This is what, in Lyons's opinion, makes it difficult for historians to disentangle the causes of the Easter Rising. Pearse was part of a conspiracy, operating secretly within a secret organisation which had itself infiltrated the Irish Volunteers. Secondly, the speech gives no clue as to the activities of Clarke and MacDermott, the principal IRB conspirators, who were using Pearse as a front man. While he could electrify the funeral crowd at Glasnevin with his oratory, Pearse was, in the words of his biographer Ruth Dudley Edwards, a solitary figure with little organisational ability. Moreover, Source 2 makes no reference to the war in Europe which had brought the old Fenian maxim, "England's difficulty is Ireland's opportunity", into much sharper focus. There is, however, a message in the speech that a blood sacrifice may well be necessary to breathe life into the spirit of Irish nationality. Indeed, the choice of a memorable phrase like "Life springs from death" highlights the involvement of romantic revolutionaries – such as Pearse, Plunkett and MacDonagh, all teachers and poets – in the IRB web planning the Easter Rising.

Source 3 illustrates Pearse's thinking on the eve of the rebellion. It is a useful document as it outlines Pearse's attempts to justify the Rising to the Irish people.

135

Reference is made to the individual groups participating in the rebellion, and it states that the insurgents have bided their time, delaying their strike until the best chance of victory. There is some hint of IRB planning, although the difficulty in securing the involvement of the Irish Volunteers, whose leader was not a revolutionary Nationalist, is glossed over. Source 3 also highlights the support that was forthcoming from the IRB's sister organisation in America, but its description of the Germans as their "gallant allies in Europe" was certain to cause anger among many citizens who had family members on the Western Front fighting against Germany. Perhaps the most significant phrase in the proclamation is the assertion that the leaders of the Rising have "full confidence of victory". Even a detached, romantic figure like Pearse must have known that he was leading his followers to certain defeat. This was clear when the plan to land German arms fell through and MacNeill issued his famous countermanding orders, but Pearse and the other leaders were prepared to press on regardless. Indirectly, therefore, Source 3 highlights the importance of the blood sacrifice belief among the IRB Military Council.

While both Sources 2 and 3 contain important details about the background to the Rising, Source 1 is the most useful. It is more wide-ranging in scope and, although written before Pearse had joined the IRB, details the route to violent revolution.

Prophetic writing?

THE RISE OF SINN FÉIN

Source 1

I have been about the country, specially in Mayo, and have had an opportunity of discussing the political situation with very many people; with Priests, Party followers, Independents and Sinn Féiners, both there and in Dublin. I feel that it is right to inform you on this matter, even if the information is disagreeable. For many reasons I am in a better position to hear the real views of the people than members of the party or their agents. In the first place practically all the young men are Sinn Féiners in more or less degree. Your speeches and actions ought to have mitigated hostility, but they have not; the prisoners and Sinn Féiners believe that the late arrests were instigated by the Party and that the speeches in the House were merely bluff. They are hostile both to the policy, the members and leaders of the Party, and would change all if possible. The older and more responsible men, as an example of whom I might take the parish priests, are gravely dissatisfied with the party policy; they desire much more vigorous action both by vote *and speech against any government that refuses Irish demands: they are not hostile to the leaders, whose past services they remember, but they would like to see them more active and determined — not in* talk *only. They have lost faith in the Home Rule Bill, and demand control over all taxation, and over trade, customs, and excise, and an abolition of concurrent legislation; these are the three main items.*

Extract from a letter from Colonel Maurice Moore to John Dillon, 4 March 1917
NLI: Maurice Moore Papers, MS 10561/9

Source 2

You are requested, by your votes, to assert before the nations of the world that Ireland's claim is to the status of an independent nation, and that we shall be satisfied with nothing less than our full claim — that in fact any scheme of government which does not confer upon the people of Ireland the supreme, absolute, and final control of all this country, external as well as internal, is a mockery and will not be accepted.

Election address by Michael Collins, December 1918
Dorothy Macardle, *The Irish Republic* (Wolfhound Press, 1999)

Source 3

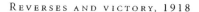

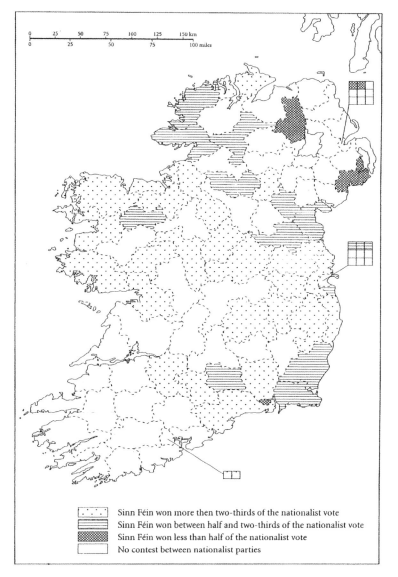

Figure 4.1 The 1918 election

From Michael Laffan, *The Resurrection of Ireland: The Sinn Féin Party 1916–1923* (Cambridge University Press, 1999)

Q1

Consult Sources 1 and 2. Explain and compare the effectiveness of the IPP and Sinn Féin parties in the 1917–18 period.

Colonel Maurice Moore's letter to Dillon presents a detailed account of the IPP's failings in the early months of 1917. His letter was written only weeks after Sinn Féin's by-election victory in North Roscommon and was meant as a wake-up call for the IPP leadership. In his claim that he is in touch with people on the ground and is, therefore, well briefed, Moore is implying that the IPP leaders have lost touch with "the real views of the people". Moreover, his insistence on providing an accurate analysis of the state of the party, even though this will be "disagreeable", suggests that the leadership has been reluctant to accept the truth on the decline of the IPP. Indeed, Moore's outlook is extremely pessimistic. He warns that "practically all the young men" are supporting Sinn Féin in spite of Dillon's valiant efforts to prevent the slide in support for the IPP. This is a reference to Dillon's spirited attempts to defend the IPP's position – which had been under severe pressure since the Easter Rising – beginning with his famous speech in the Commons on 11 May 1916, when he had attacked the British government for ruining the achievements of the IPP. From Moore's report, however, it is clear that the public no longer trusts the IPP, even Dillon whose speeches are seen as "bluff", and the party has great difficulty in refuting Sinn Féin allegations of collusion between the IPP and the British government. A further criticism of the IPP's ineffectiveness is contained in Moore's observation that even the Catholic clergy and the older generation, the party's core supporters, are unhappy at the IPP's performance. They want a change in party policy which will require a sustained onslaught on the government and the provision of a new constitutional settlement that will go beyond Home Rule to give a Dublin parliament greater powers. The only glimmer of hope for the IPP in Moore's report is his description of the respect in which the leaders are still held for their "past services". It was, of course, this cohort of leaders who had led the campaign of agrarian agitation that had eventually won the right of ownership of the land for the tenant farming class. These same leaders had kept alive the demand for Home Rule and appeared to have delivered a successful outcome in 1914, but the events of the war and the Easter Rising had undermined the IPP's position. At the same time, the leadership was ageing and, from Moore's report, was much less active and effective than it had been in the past. This was in sharp contrast to the energy, dynamism and enthusiasm of the youthful Sinn Féin leadership. Although historians disagree on the strength of the IPP at the outbreak of the war, there is no doubt that Redmond had been damaged by the Ulster crisis, and his position became more vulnerable as the war dragged on. Furthermore, his participation in the abortive Lloyd George peace initiative in the weeks after the Rising left the IPP leader an easy target for militant Nationalism. Moore was a loyal supporter of the IPP, but his letter highlights the party's failings. His warning that a complete change of course would be necessary to instil confidence among IPP supporters indicates the seriousness of the situation for the IPP in the early part of 1917.

Michael Collins's address to his supporters in South County Cork before the general election in December 1918 illustrates the confidence of a powerful Sinn Féin party. Sinn Féin policy is clearly stated, and the message given is that there will be no compromise with a Westminster government on the issue of freedom. There is, therefore, implied criticism of IPP compromises in recent years, most notably the concessions made by Redmond in the Lloyd George peace initiative of 1916 and the Irish Convention of 1917–18. Indeed, there is no specific reference to the IPP, as it is apparently dismissed as an irrelevance by Collins. While he does not use the term republic, it is clear that Collins regards the 1918 general election as a referendum on Irish freedom. Irish voters are being asked to "assert" Irish independence "before the nations of the world". This quest for international recognition of Ireland's independence was important for Sinn Féin, and it chimed with the party's policy of appealing for Irish independence at the post-war Peace Conference. Of course, Collins had first-hand knowledge of Sinn Féin's powerful electoral machine in which the Volunteers played an active role. While the party was very popular with younger voters, Michael Laffan has highlighted contemporary anecdotal evidence, suggesting that sons often pressurised their fathers into voting for Sinn Féin. The 1918 general election was also the first election to be fought under universal suffrage, as all men over 21 and all women over 30 now had the right to vote. This change had the effect of trebling the franchise in Ireland, thereby creating a large voting bloc with no party allegiance. Not surprisingly, the great majority of these first-time voters were attracted by a youthful, dynamic party which had established a local Sinn Féin club in almost every parish in Ireland. In his address Collins states succinctly that Sinn Féin will not accept any scheme that threatens Irish unity; in their determination to emphasise their opposition to conscription, Sinn Féin leaders such as Collins and de Valera were nominated as candidates for seats in Ulster.

By December 1918, as Collins's address indicates, Sinn Féin was the dominant force in Nationalist Ireland and was supremely confident of victory. The Easter Rising had fatally damaged the IPP and radicalised Irish Nationalism, a development that was reflected in the growth of Sinn Féin. The IPP's ailing organisation, which was in difficulty everywhere outside Ulster, was no match for the vibrant, efficient Sinn Féin movement.

Q2

Consult all the sources. How far do they suggest that Sinn Féin's landslide victory in December 1918 was due to the collapse of the IPP?

Source 1 highlights the weaknesses of the IPP approximately 20 months before the 1918 general election, and from March 1917 the IPP faced further problems which contributed to its calamitous defeat in the post-war election. The IPP had been in serious trouble since the Rising, and Dillon was desperately trying to shore up support. From his contacts with grass-roots opinion Colonel Moore warns Dillon that the party is struggling to hold onto its traditional support. In its early phase the IPP had been the party of the tenant farming class, but its success in cajoling successive Westminster governments into conceding land ownership had cost the IPP its social base. While the Irish electorate, as Moore points out, has not forgotten the "past services" of the party's leaders, there is obvious anger at the IPP's failure to conduct a more vigorous campaign on behalf of Nationalist Ireland. Without the land question the IPP could only focus on the quest for Home Rule, but the party was clearly in a state of limbo after September 1914, when the Home Rule Act was put on the statute book. While Home Rule was, therefore, tantalisingly close, the IPP could not escape the frustration of the 'post-dated cheque'. These "older and more responsible men" want the party to take a firm stance against current British policy in Ireland, which has alienated public opinion with its reaction to the Rising. They want more independence than Home Rule can offer, and their criticism of the party focuses on its inaction and lack of initiative. Clearly, the IPP had been overwhelmed by recent events and was unable to adapt to the changed circumstances of 1917–18. Further evidence of the IPP's impending collapse appears in Moore's observation that "practically all the young men" have been attracted to the new Sinn Féin party. These young men do not trust the IPP and are "hostile" to it, as they are constantly reminded of Redmond's support for the British war effort by Sinn Féin propaganda. Moore's pessimistic tone appears to offer little hope of an IPP recovery; it is clear that Moore believes the party has its head in the sand and is even unwilling to give serious consideration to its predicament. This reflects reality, because the party lacked the energy and organisational structure to withstand the challenge of a dynamic Sinn Féin movement.

Source 2, on the other hand, does not deal with the failings of the IPP. In fact, Collins's election address makes no mention of IPP opposition, and this is indicative of Sinn Féin's dismissive attitude to the IPP by December 1918. Collins makes a bold, confident statement, asserting Ireland's right to independence and calling on the electorate to support Sinn Féin's stance. Moreover, in his reference to "the nations of the world", Collins is highlighting the significance of winning *self determination.*

international recognition for a new independent Ireland. This had featured prominently in Sinn Féin's election manifesto which pledged that the party would present the case for Irish independence at the post-war Peace Conference. Source 2 also includes indirect criticism of the IPP's Ulster policy, as Collins demands that independence should be on the basis of a United Ireland. Overall, however, Collins's address does not support the view that Sinn Féin's landslide victory was due to the collapse of the IPP. Instead, as Michael Laffan has argued, Irish Nationalism had undergone a rapid process of radicalisation in the post-Rising period, and Sinn Féin accurately reflected and benefited from this development.

Source 3, the electoral map, provides clear evidence of both the IPP's collapse and of Sinn Féin's strength. A striking feature of the map is the large number of uncontested seats – 25 in all, which is evidence of the scale of the IPP's demoralisation by December 1918. This was particularly true in Munster, where the IPP, having won these seats in the previous election, simply abandoned large areas of the province. Dillon himself lamented the poor state of the party's organisation throughout the country, but in conceding so many seats to Sinn Féin without even token resistance the IPP surrendered the opportunity to offer a choice to the large number of first-time voters. These men and women were eligible to vote on the extended franchise of 1918. Only in North East Ulster, where the IPP had always been confronted by a powerful and well organised Unionist party, did the IPP's much more efficient organisation give them the chance of electoral success. Yet even here, four of the party's six victories were primarily due to an electoral pact brokered by Cardinal Logue, who had feared that a split Nationalist vote would allow Unionist candidates to win seats that had Catholic majorities. Only in Waterford City and in Falls (Belfast) did the IPP secure victory in a straight fight with Sinn Féin. Waterford returned John Redmond's son, as the family retained its popularity in the area, while Joe Devlin defeated de Valera in Falls. Here the Ancient Order of Hibernians (AOH) provided Devlin with the organisational support necessary to mobilise the IPP vote. Elsewhere, however, the map illustrates the dominance and electoral appeal of the new Sinn Féin party and emphasises that the IPP was a spent force by the end of the war.

Therefore, Sources 1 and 3 point to the IPP's collapse, while Source 2 is evidence of a confident Sinn Féin which expects a landslide victory in the general election.

Q3

Consult all the sources. Which of them would a historian value most in a study of the rise of Sinn Féin in the 1917–18 period?

All three of the sources would prove useful to a historian studying the rise of Sinn Féin following the Easter Rising.

Source 1 is a very useful document. Written by a leading Redmondite who had served as Inspector-General of the National Volunteers, the letter catalogues the problems facing the IPP in the early part of 1917. While Moore was a party loyalist and was desperate for the IPP to arrest its decline, the pessimistic tone of the letter is striking. Obviously, Moore cannot foresee an IPP recovery. His warning that "practically all the young men are Sinn Féiners" is evidence of a generational divide that was emerging in Nationalist Ireland after the Rising. For these young men Sinn Féin was perceived as a youthful, dynamic party, and this contrasted sharply with the IPP's image as an ageing, ineffective political movement. Moore is implying that while the IPP engages in "talk only", Sinn Féin is a party of action. This is an accurate reflection of the transformation that had taken place in contemporary Irish politics. As Michael Laffan has noted, Irish Nationalism was in the process of radicalisation, and Moore, who is able to gauge opinion at grass-roots level, is an eyewitness to this development. His reference to County Mayo is significant, because it bordered the Westminster constituency of North Roscommon, which had just seen Sinn Féin's first by-election victory in the previous month. There, Count Plunkett's policy of abstention from Westminster had chimed perfectly with the new republican Nationalism that was developing in the months following the Rising. Moreover, Moore's warning that the IPP is losing touch with its core support, including the parish priests, is evidence that the party cannot connect with even the older voters who had supported it since the 1880s. While these people are indebted to the IPP for its success on the land question, they are clearly frustrated by the party's failure to respond to the new circumstances of 1917–18. Even the immediate implementation of Home Rule will not satisfy this group, demonstrating that Redmond's pro-war, pro-British strategy had undermined the party's position, particularly after the Easter Rising. If the electorate demanded a much greater level of independence than that conferred by the Home Rule Bill, then switching support to Sinn Féin was a logical development. Moore's analysis of the current position in March 1917 offers a devastating critique of the IPP's weaknesses and holds out little prospect of this trend being reversed. This makes it an invaluable document for a historian studying the rise of Sinn Féin in 1917–18. Moore's assertion that his correspondence reflects "the real views of the people" is further evidence that the party has lost touch with its electorate.

143

Source 2 is less useful in explaining Sinn Féin's success. Collins's election address presents Sinn Féin's policy in a succinct message. It demands full independence for a 32-county state and will accept nothing less. Sinn Féin aims to secure international recognition for an independent Ireland, and it states that there will be no negotiation with the British on Ireland's right to self-determination. While it does not mention a 'republic', it is clear from the address that the achievement of a republic is Sinn Féin's ultimate objective. Yet the party could also attract the support of the disgruntled former IPP supporters, described in Source 1, who simply wanted as much independence as possible. Obviously, Collins is anticipating a sweeping victory for Sinn Féin in the general election, and the IPP's failure to field candidates in so many Munster constituencies can only have increased his confidence. Although Sinn Féin had lost three successive by-elections to the IPP in the early part of 1918, the subsequent conscription crisis had the effect of rubber-stamping Sinn Féin's dominance of Nationalist Ireland. Moreover, the fact that Labour did not stand in the general election ensured that the focus would be on the national question, and this explains the nature of Collins's address. By 1917–18, as Laffan has argued, Sinn Féin had emerged as an umbrella organisation that became home to a number of militant Nationalist groups, all of which shared the common aim of ending the IPP's hegemony.

Source 3 is a very revealing document. It highlights both Sinn Féin dominance by December 1918 and the IPP's dwindling support that Moore had described in Source 1. The large number of uncontested seats, which was due to the IPP's failure to field candidates in what had mostly been safe Nationalist seats, provides clear evidence of the party's poor state by December 1918. It had abandoned 25 constituencies without putting up a fight and had conceded defeat in the general election. The extension of the franchise, creating a large number of first-time voters, had worked to Sinn Féin's advantage, while the IPP struggled to retain the support of the older voters referred to in Source 1. The conscription crisis had created a Nationalist coalition in which Sinn Féin played the leading role, and the anti-conscription campaign saw the Catholic hierarchy working closely with de Valera and the other Sinn Féin leaders. This ensured that Sinn Féin shed the image of a dangerous revolutionary party which existed in some quarters, and acquired a new respectability that proved very important in conservative, rural Ireland. Source 3 demonstrates that nearly all constituencies outside Ulster saw Sinn Féin winning more than two-thirds of the Nationalist vote, and it can be assumed that this figure would have been higher in the uncontested seats. Only in Waterford City and in Falls, where Devlin's electoral machine functioned smoothly, did the IPP score significant successes. While Dillon polled respectably in his contest with de Valera in East Mayo, the map highlights Sinn Féin's dominance in the three Southern provinces. Of course, the IPP's other four successes in Ulster were the result of a pact which ensured that seats with Catholic majorities did not fall into Unionist hands, with four being allocated to Sinn Féin and four to the IPP. Therefore, the final tally of six seats does not fully reflect the IPP's shocking weakness by December 1918. The general election results also left the Unionist party with 26 seats, nearly all of them in Ulster.

While Source 3 offers striking visual evidence of Sinn Féin's dominance over the IPP and is more useful than Source 2, it is not as useful as Source 1. In the wake of Sinn Féin's first by-election success, Moore's detailed analysis outlines the reasons for the IPP's dwindling support and points to a difficult future for Redmond's party now that it faces a powerful challenge for its control of Nationalist Ireland.

ANGLO-IRISH WAR

Source 1

In these circumstances the Government determined on the double policy which I propose now to declare. On the one hand they feel they have no option but to continue and indeed intensify their campaign against that small but highly organised and desperate minority who are using murder and outrage … but on the other hand they are anxious to open every channel … for an honourable settlement …

We have decided to proclaim in that quarter of Ireland [the South West] martial law, and to mete out exactly the same treatment to these people as would be done if they were open rebels … We are only meting out the ordinary rules of civilised warfare … There will be a proclamation of martial law … The effect will be that after a certain date unauthorised persons found in possession of arms in the specified areas to which martial law is applied will be treated as rebels, and will be liable on conviction by a military court to the penalty of death. The same penalty will be applied to the unauthorised wearing of the uniforms of any of His Majesty's forces and to the aiding and abetting and harbouring of rebels …

Extract from Lloyd George's statement to the House of Commons, 10 December 1920
HC Deb 5th series, vol 135

Source 2

In opening the latest discussion on the Irish situation in the House of Lords, the Archbishop of Canterbury took occasion once more to protest strongly against the deplorable practice of indiscriminate and unauthorised reprisals by the irregular forces of the crown. He did so on the highest of all grounds – namely, the absolute unlawfulness of the attempt to overcome wrong, however flagrant and provocative, by means of further and equally indefensible wrong. With that protest we, the undersigned, desire earnestly to associate ourselves …

In these circumstances we join our voices with those who are appealing from many sides for the adoption of a different line of policy. We plead with the Government to arrange, if possible, a genuine truce, with a view to a

---

deliberate effort after an agreed solution to the Irish difficulty. It may be that attempt will fail; but until it has been seriously and patiently tried we cannot acquiesce in any alternative course of action. The present policy is causing grave unrest throughout the Empire, and exposing us to misunderstanding and the hostile criticism even of the most friendly of other nations of the world … It affords no prospect of the speedy restoration of law and order.

Extract from a declaration issued by 7 Church of England bishops and 13 leaders of other Protestant churches in England and Scotland
Published in the English press, 6 April 1921

Source 3

The British decision to negotiate a truce represented an uncomfortable acknowledgement of realities and also the dominance of political over purely military considerations. The option of martial law for the whole of Ireland and a vast stepping-up of troop numbers had proved unpalatable.

From both Irish and British perspectives, the logic behind a cessation of hostilities meant that the achievement of a settlement became imperative. Any successful compromise was to be on the lines suggested in the earlier peace initiatives.

From Michael Hopkinson, *The Irish War of Independence* (Gill and Macmillan, 2002)

Q1

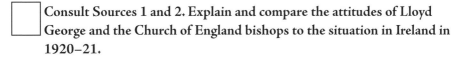

Consult Sources 1 and 2. Explain and compare the attitudes of Lloyd George and the Church of England bishops to the situation in Ireland in 1920–21.

In Source 1 Lloyd George, the British Prime Minister, is informing the House of Commons of the present security situation in Ireland and is outlining the Coalition government's plans for tackling IRA violence. The statement came just days after Bloody Sunday and the Kilmichael ambush in County Cork, incidents which marked an escalation of the conflict. Lloyd George is determined that the Crown Forces in Ireland should pursue their objective of a military victory over the IRA. In fact, the recent upsurge in republican violence has resulted in the Prime Minister's decision to "intensify" the campaign against the IRA; as the historian Robert Kee has noted, the final phase of the war from November 1920 to July 1921 was the "harshest phase", when the number of casualties on both sides rose sharply. In spite of the failure on British military policy up to December 1920, Lloyd George was confident that the IRA would be defeated. In his Commons' speech he describes the active Volunteers as a "small" and "desperate minority", indicating that he remains confident a final push could achieve success, although he does acknowledge that the enemy is "highly organised". For the Prime Minister, victory would be achieved by imposing martial law in four counties in the South West, which had experienced most of the violence. By this stage both the Black and Tans and the Auxiliaries were up to their required numbers, and it was the government's intention to use these forces to take the fight to the enemy. Lloyd George's statement that "We are only meting out the ordinary rules of civilised warfare" would have convinced no one in Ireland, where the population in the proclaimed areas frequently witnessed and were sometimes victims of the policy of reprisals – to which the government had given its tacit approval. Indeed, support for the government's security policy was evaporating rapidly in England, as the press and other groups intensified their attacks on the Coalition government's strategy. Lloyd George's speech demonstrates that the government intended to fight terror by applying the death penalty – through a system of military courts – to those found guilty of possessing arms, wearing the uniforms of Crown Forces, or "aiding and abetting and harbouring" the rebels. Therefore, Lloyd George was determined to increase the pressure on the IRA by deploying additional resources, proclaiming martial law in the worst trouble spots and introducing tougher security measures. Yet, at the same time, the Prime Minister is emphasising that he has a "double policy". While he intends to intensify the military campaign against the IRA, Lloyd George expresses his intention to pursue a political solution by opening "every channel … for an honourable settlement". Already, peace feelers had been issued with government approval, and Archbishop Clune, an Australian Catholic cleric who was anxious to end the violence in Ireland, was in contact with republican leaders and with Lloyd George himself in his attempts to broker a truce. Although these efforts failed, it provided evidence that the government had given at least some consideration to the possibility of reaching a political settlement with Sinn Féin. On the other hand, Conservative members of the Coalition government still favoured coercion, and they regarded Sinn Féin's willingness to consider a truce as a sign of weakness, encouraging them to give wholehearted support to a renewed military effort in Ireland. In these circumstances, while Lloyd George expresses his support for a political option in December 1920, he was to change his mind once Conservative and military opposition became apparent.

Source 2, the declaration by the Church of England bishops, paints a very different view of the situation in Ireland. In the four months since the Prime Minister's statement in the Commons the conflict in Ireland had become a much bloodier affair, as the government's moves to force a military breakthrough added to the number of violent engagements. The bishops are appalled by the actions of Crown Forces, and they are outraged by the "reprisals" carried out by the "irregular forces of the crown" – a clear reference to the activities of the Black and Tans and the Auxiliaries. These reprisals, which were repeatedly being used in response to IRA outrages are referred to as "indiscriminate and unauthorised". The bishops also refer to the Archbishop of Canterbury's protest in the House of Lords, when he stressed the "absolute unlawfulness" of attempting to meet "wrong" with "wrong". In contrast to Source 1, the bishops are demanding a shift in government policy and an end to military hostilities. They want a truce followed by a freely negotiated political settlement. Such criticism of the government's military policy in Ireland had mounted in the early part of 1921, as the level of violence increased dramatically. The Labour Party, the Asquithian Liberals, the Trade Union movement and the bulk of the press had joined the Anglican Church in its condemnation of British policy. The bishops also warn that the present policy in Ireland is provoking international outrage, particularly in the British Empire, where it had the capacity to cause lasting damage. There was even criticism from Britain's erstwhile ally, the United States, and the bishops are pleading with the government to change course before it is too late. Significantly, they disagree with Lloyd George's earlier assessment of the prospect of military victory in Ireland. They argue that the present policy offers no hope of "the speedy restoration of law and order", and that it will definitely fail to lay the foundations for the ultimate objective of a peaceful and contented Ireland. Since the autumn of 1920 even *The Times*, normally a staunch supporter of government policy in Ireland, had begun to express grave concern about the policy of reprisals and the damage caused to Britain's reputation. By April 1921, with the deterioration of the security situation in Ireland, the Coalition government was coming under increasing pressure to end its policy of reprisals and embark on a quest for a political solution to the Irish problem. The bishops' revulsion at present policy accurately mirrored public opinion and was to force Lloyd George into a major political climbdown within a few months, when he began planning for a truce with republican forces.

There are clear differences between Lloyd George's approach to the situation in Ireland and the attitude taken by the Church of England bishops.

Q2

Consult all the sources. How far do they suggest that the British government had little alternative but to seek a truce in 1921?

While Source 1 indicates that the British government was "anxious to open every channel" for a political settlement, this was clearly not the preferred option of the Cabinet at the end of 1920. Although Lloyd George was aware of a number of clandestine contacts aimed at laying the ground for a truce, his Commons' speech in December 1920 provides ample evidence of his belief that a major security crackdown would lead to victory over the IRA. From the outset Lloyd George viewed the actions of IRA Volunteers as criminal activities, and he regarded the apprehension of these criminals as a policeman's job. When RIC numbers began to fall in response to the IRA's campaign of intimidation, the Coalition government chose to reinforce the RIC rather than deploy large numbers of troops. By December 1920, moreover, the Prime Minister refused to recognise that a small war was going on in Ireland, and he continued to argue that this "desperate minority" was guilty of serious crime. The government, he claims, has no alternative but to "continue and indeed intensify" the campaign against the IRA. By imposing martial law in the most violent areas and using military courts against those suspected of helping the Volunteers, Lloyd George expresses his confidence in a successful outcome. Indeed, he was convinced that the systematic use of reprisals was the only way to tackle opponents that he described as a "murder gang". Just a few weeks before his Commons' speech Lloyd George's confidence of victory in Ireland led to his famous declaration that they had "murder by the throat", and Source 1 indicates that he believed a successful military outcome was certainly achievable. Like any successful political leader, however, Lloyd George was always open to new initiatives, and this is why he approved of an exploration of the peace feelers that Sinn Féin had sent out in the autumn of 1920. Yet, while he endorsed the idea of a peace process, he was not committed to the principle of a truce in December 1920, believing that military victory was well within his government's grasp.

The bishops' statement in Source 2 suggests that there was little prospect of military victory, and with criticism of the government's Irish policy mounting Lloyd George had no alternative but to negotiate a truce with the republican leadership. The declaration expresses revulsion at the unofficial reprisals carried out by the Black and Tans and Auxiliaries and claims that the use of "indefensible wrong" to tackle IRA violence is both morally wrong and militarily ineffective. The bishops advocate a change of direction by the government. They want a truce as a precondition for genuine negotiations leading to a political settlement between Britain and Ireland. While they acknowledge that such an initiative might prove unsuccessful, the bishops insist that a truce and subsequent negotiations must be tried, because they "cannot acquiesce in any alternative course of action". The bishops argue that there is no alternative, as the present policy of coercion is turning opinion against the government in a way that can no longer be ignored. Opposition to the policy of reprisals was mounting throughout the Empire, and the bishops were joined in their condemnation of government policy by a host of organisations in Britain. With no prospect of a speedy restoration of law and order in Ireland, the bishops are convinced that the government must abandon repression, which is proving counterproductive, and conclude a truce with the IRA before embarking on negotiations with the republican leadership.

Source 3, an extract from Michael Hopkinson's book on the War of Independence, also supports the view that the British had no alternative but to seek a truce in July 1921. While this represented an embarrassing U-turn for the government, and in particular for Lloyd George, the British were forced to accept "an uncomfortable acknowledgement of realities". Indeed, as the historian Lord Longford has noted, it took an impressive debate in Cabinet to persuade the Prime Minister of the wisdom of agreeing to a truce as a prelude to negotiations between the British government and Sinn Féin representatives. By the summer of 1921 it had become apparent to military commanders that the establishment of martial law would be required over all 26 counties in the South, if the government hoped to quell the violence. This would have required approximately 200,000 troops, and there was little enthusiasm for such a strategy at Westminster. Hopkinson also emphasises the political pressures that had pushed the Lloyd George government in the direction of truce. Ironically, by the end of the war the British were beginning to come to grips with the IRA's guerrilla campaign, but just when it appeared that the British were in sight of military victory the political will to continue the struggle evaporated. This was due to the internal political pressure and international criticism which the government suffered in the final phase of the conflict. Of course, for a cessation of hostilities to take place both sides had to agree to the truce, and Source 3 indicates that the Irish as well as the British had good cause to support the truce option in 1921. By this stage, as Collins subsequently admitted, the IRA was finding it difficult to sustain its guerrilla campaign, while the people's increasing war weariness in crucial areas such as West Cork and South Tipperary made a truce a much more welcome alternative to the Volunteers.

Therefore, Source 1 suggests that while the government was willing to consider a political alternative, it was firmly concentrating on the steps necessary to achieve military success. Sources 2 and 3, on the other hand, demonstrate that there was no alternative for the Coalition government other than to conclude a truce and open negotiations for a political settlement.

Q3

Consult all the sources. Which of them would a historian value most in assessing British policy in Ireland in 1920–21?

All three sources would be useful for a historian studying British policy in Ireland in the 1920–21 period.

The War of Independence began in January 1919, although in its first year it is more accurate to describe events in Ireland as sporadic violence rather than a small war. From the beginning Lloyd George regarded the conflict as a policeman's job, and this led the government to introduce the Black and Tans and Auxiliaries in an attempt to reinforce the RIC. Almost immediately, both of these forces were engaged in controversial incidents which highlighted their indiscipline. At the same time the IRA developed its use of flying columns – armed groups of about 25 men who lived on the run – and the level of violence increased significantly. Source 1 describes the Prime Minister's thinking on the Irish situation as the war entered its bloodiest phase at the end of 1920. Lloyd George claimed he was dealing with a "murder gang", and in his Commons' speech he tells the House that they have to "intensify" the campaign against the IRA. Source 1 clearly illustrates the Prime Minister's confidence in ultimate victory and his belief that the establishment of martial law in the four most violent counties of the South West would give the Crown Forces an advantage. This was to be accompanied by draconian security measures, which would increase the pressure on IRA flying columns and their supporters. The Prime Minister's speech was very significant, because it came just days after Bloody Sunday and the Kilmichael ambush – brutal engagements which led to an escalation of the conflict. In the circumstances Lloyd George argues that his government has "no option" but to respond to the upsurge in IRA violence with more coercion. This support for repression also reflects the wishes of the Conservative members of his Cabinet, and although Lloyd George is personally in favour of intensifying military operations in Ireland, he is flexible enough to inform MPs that his government is exploring "every channel" in an effort to find a political settlement. Source 1 is a valuable document because it highlights Lloyd George's determination to pursue the military option at the end of 1920, despite the fact that public opinion in Britain was beginning to question the British campaign in Ireland.

Source 2 provides an excellent overview of the criticism being levelled at the Coalition government at a time when the policy of reprisals was attracting unwelcome international attention. The bishops express their revulsion at the brutality of the "irregular forces" being deployed by the British government, claiming that no provocation, "however flagrant and provocative", could justify such bloody reprisals. These leading figures in the Church of England are outraged at actions such as the burning of Cork City by the Auxiliaries on 11 December 1920, and they are angry that such activities have tarnished the good name of Britain in the international community. The Anglican bishops insist that the government must abandon military repression and pursue a "different line of policy". This is a useful document because it reflects the swing in public opinion during the early part of 1921. The bishops were joined by the Labour Party, Asquith and his Liberal followers, the TUC, and a new non-party pressure group the Peace with Ireland Council, in demanding a change in government policy. All of these groups sought to apply moral pressure on the Lloyd George government, but the Anglican bishops proved the most effective in this objective. By this stage, moreover, the British press, with the exception of the right wing *Morning Post*, had joined together to denounce the failure of British policy and urge a political alternative. Source 2 is a very valuable document as it offers an excellent example of the reason for the shift in public opinion which soon forced Lloyd George to accept a truce in July 1921. Although the British had a clear military advantage by the summer of 1921, the political will to continue the conflict had dried up, and it was the actions of the Anglican bishops as described in Source 2 that did much to swing public opinion against government policy.

Source 3 presents an accurate summary of the reasons behind the Coalition government's change of policy. While Lloyd George had consistently argued that he would not negotiate with the "murder gang", he found himself advocating a U-turn once he finally recognised that British security policy had been a spectacular failure. Hopkinson records that this decision had been made with great reluctance, suggesting that it had taken the British government a considerable time to acknowledge "realities" in Ireland. He also explains correctly that the decision to negotiate a truce had been taken for political, not military, reasons. This was a reference to the pressure, both internal and external, that the government had been put under as criticism of the government's security policy gathered pace in 1921. Lloyd George had been informed by his military commanders that the army should play the lead role if military victory remained an objective, but that this would require martial law throughout the 26 counties and the deployment of 200,000 troops. As Hopkinson notes, the government found such a prospect "unpalatable". Source 3 is also more wide-ranging in scope. It mentions that both the Irish and British had sound reasons for agreeing to a truce, and, furthermore, the desire to find a political settlement had become "imperative" for both sides. On the British side the political will to continue the conflict no longer existed, while on the Irish side the IRA was struggling to sustain its military campaign in some areas, where war weariness among the local population was already a recognisable feature.

Undoubtedly, Bonar Law's resignation from the Coalition government in March 1921 had given Lloyd George more room to manoeuvre, but it still took a great effort on the part of other Cabinet ministers to persuade Lloyd George to change course on Ireland. Yet, once this had been achieved the Prime Minister moved quickly on the political front, holding out the carrot of dominion status to Sinn Féin representatives.

Therefore, Source 3, written by an acknowledged expert on the subject, is a valuable summary of the reasons for agreement on a truce. Source 1 is also useful, as it illustrates Lloyd George's determination and commitment to the military option, even though the conflict in Ireland had escalated; it also offers the prospect, however slight, of a political option. While Sources 1 and 3 are both extremely useful, Source 2 would be of most value to a historian assessing British policy in 1920–21. It outlines the reasons for the failure of British security policy and highlights the pressure on the government, which eventually led them to concede a truce and political negotiations.

THE TREATY

Source 1

The British delegates were fully aware of the strengths and weaknesses of their own position when they entered the conference room on 11 October. They were convinced that, as far as British public opinion was concerned, 'loyalty to the Throne and Empire would command universal acceptance', and could, if necessary, be made an issue of peace or war. But they were equally convinced that if the Irish plenipotentiaries postponed acceptance of allegiance to the Crown until they had ascertained British policy towards Ulster, then the government could not rely upon the British public to give it full support. The particular difficulty concerned the border counties of Tyrone and Fermanagh, which had small but distinct Nationalist majorities, but which had none the less been placed under the jurisdiction of the Northern Ireland parliament.

**From David George Boyce, *Englishmen and Irish Troubles: British Public Opinion and the Making of Irish Policy 1918–22*
(Jonathan Cape, 1972)**

Source 2

The delegation again returned to Dublin on 2 December and went into session with the cabinet on the following day. The meeting demonstrated that the only remaining major stumbling-block to an agreement was the form of the oath of allegiance. It also revealed that the delegation was split. Barton and Duffy, as well as Childers, believed more could be extracted from the British, while Griffith, Collins and Duggan basically did not. Both Brugha and Collins objected to the wording of the proposed oath of allegiance, but Collins pointed out that it would not come into effect for twelve months, and he asked if it 'would be worth while taking that twelve months and seeing how it would work'. De Valera and Brugha objected to the provisions for the North, which included a Boundary Commission. In his characteristically blunt fashion, Brugha addressed the matter of the division in the delegation. He wanted to know 'who was responsible for the splitting of the Delegation so that two members (Messrs Griffith and Collins) did most of the work and that the other members were not in possession of full information'. He was told that 'the British Government *was responsible for the arrangement but that it had the approval of the whole Delegation'. Brugha's response was that 'the British Government selected its men'.*

From Arthur Mitchell, *Revolutionary Government in Ireland: Dail Eireann 1919–22* (Gill and Macmillan, 1993)

Source 3

On my return from London, when it became necessary to send a written reply to the British proposals, I proposed another way out – external association of Ireland with the group of free nations in the British Empire ... In entering such an association Ireland would be doing nothing incompatible with her declared independence ... This proposal in its main outline was accepted by the [Dáil] Cabinet and the whole Ministry (about 15 members were present when I made it) and I set out with the fixed determination of making peace on that basis. Lest I might in any way compromise the position of the Republic, and in order that I might be in a position to meet any tricks of Lloyd George, I remained at home myself, but the plenipotentiaries had agreed with my view, had had their instructions and even a preliminary draft treaty to guide them.

Extract from a letter from De Valera to Joseph McGarrity, 21 December 1921
Seán Cronin, *The McGarrity Papers* (Anvil Books, 1972)

Q1

Consult Sources 1 and 2. Explain and compare the problems facing the respective delegations during the Treaty negotiations.

Sources 1 and 2 highlight the problems facing both the British and Irish delegations at different stages of the Treaty negotiations in the final months of 1921.

At the outset, Source 1 reveals the British delegates' belief that public opinion was firmly behind them in defending the position of Crown and Empire during the negotiations. Furthermore, the delegation was confident that it could threaten war on these issues if the Irish refused to recognise the Crown and come into the Empire. On entering the negotiations, therefore, the British delegates were convinced that public opinion in Britain would support the reopening of the war on these issues. This was despite the fact that it had been public outrage over the conduct of the War of Independence that had been the crucial factor in persuading the

Lloyd George government to accept a truce, followed by negotiations with Sinn Féin. Naturally, this could be viewed as a trump card and, throughout the negotiations, Lloyd George never abandoned the alternative of war which, the Sinn Féin delegates were subtly reminded, would be the consequence of a conference breakdown. This obvious advantage was, however, balanced by the British delegation's sense of weakness on the Ulster question. Source 1 demonstrates the Westminster government's anxiety regarding Ulster, fearing that it would present major difficulties once negotiations were under way. Lloyd George and his colleagues fully expected the Irish delegation to use the Ulster issue and exploit this weakness. The logical strategy that Sinn Féin would follow was to make acceptance of the Crown and Empire conditional on the ending of partition, and the British government undoubtedly anticipated little assistance from the Unionist government in Belfast in any attempt to square this particular circle. If Lloyd George was confident that public opinion in Britain would support the reopening of the war on the basis of Crown and Empire, he was equally convinced that his Coalition government could not rely on the same support with Ulster as the prize. Moreover, the Prime Minister had just learnt a bitter lesson during the War of Independence – that retaliation against Ireland which did not have public backing must end in failure. In particular, Source 1 focuses on the "difficulty" of Tyrone and Fermanagh, two counties that were now part of Northern Ireland but had Nationalist majorities. This made it especially difficult for the British government to defend partition, and yet Lloyd George also had to be mindful of his dependence on Conservative support to keep his shaky Coalition government in power. Many of these Conservatives, notably Lord Birkenhead, a key member of his negotiating team, were adamant that the Unionist government should not be coerced into accepting any loss of territory. While the bond between the Conservatives and the Ulster Unionists was clearly not as strong as it had been in the 1912–14 period, there remained sufficient goodwill on the part of the Tories to shield the Unionist government from Westminster pressure, and Lloyd George knew this.

Source 2 captures the difficulties facing the Irish delegation, as the negotiations entered their final phase. Although the passage claims that the only obstacle to a treaty was the wording of the oath of allegiance, it also acknowledges that the Irish delegation "was split". Among the delegates, Barton and Duffy – who were supported by Childers, the secretary to the Sinn Féin delegation – believed that the British would, if pressurised, make further concessions, particularly on the crucial issue of national status. On the other side, Griffith, Collins and Duggan were convinced that the draft Treaty, which they had brought to Dublin for discussion at Cabinet level, represented the crux of the final British offer. These three, particularly Collins, feared that the rejection of the key British proposals could spark the resumption of war in Ireland, and the likely defeat of the IRA. This meeting of the Cabinet on Saturday, 3 December 1921 also witnessed the eruption of fierce arguments between a number of leading figures in the Sinn Féin government. At this dramatic meeting, Brugha, the Minister of Defence, launched a scathing personal attack on Griffith and Collins, whom he blamed for making unnecessary concessions as they negotiated with the British at sub-conference level. Yet even Collins and his arch-enemy, Brugha, were in agreement in their objection to the oath of allegiance as worded in the draft proposals, but the pragmatic Collins argued that it should be given a trial period. Significantly, the oath remained a crucial difficulty even after seven weeks of negotiations, and this ultimately was the issue that was primarily responsible for the subsequent Treaty split. Brugha and Collins were also united in their apprehension over the draft Treaty's failure to deal decisively with the border question. Yet the Dáil debates on the actual Treaty during the next few weeks indicated that the limitations of the proposed Boundary Commission were largely ignored by Dáil deputies, who preferred to focus on the oath of allegiance. Even de Valera's Document No. 2 virtually repeated word-for-word the Boundary Commission proposals, although Collins was secretly intent on using political and military pressure in order to end partition. Beyond the bitter personal divisions revealed at this highly charged meeting of the Dáil Cabinet, Source 2 indicates that the Irish delegation was not only split on the question of the oath but was also nervous about the last stage of the negotiations. With the British pressing for a response Barton even suggested that de Valera should accompany the delegation for the closing phase of the negotiations, but the Sinn Féin leader did not deem this late intervention necessary. Of course, the divisions within the Irish delegation mirrored a wider division in the broader Sinn Féin party which had emerged as an umbrella movement in 1917. In fact, the Dáil government had deliberately put together a divided delegation to conduct negotiations on its behalf, and this naturally became a major problem for Griffith, who led the Irish delegation. Indeed, Lloyd George quickly recognised this, and he exploited these divisions to his advantage.

There is, therefore, a major contrast in the two sources. While the British were clear on their objectives and united in the pursuit of these goals, they were also fully aware of their strengths and weaknesses. This is borne out in Source 1. The Irish, on the other hand, were obviously divided, and they lacked a clear strategy, beyond exploiting the British embarrassment over partition, for extracting concessions from the British. This situation was exacerbated, because the Irish delegation had failed to reach agreement on the key issue of national status before leaving for London.

Q2

Consult all the sources. How far do they suggest that external association was a likely outcome of the Treaty negotiations?

Although only Source 3 makes a direct reference to "external association", Sources 1 and 2 deal with issues of Ireland's national status which have a major bearing on the prospects for external association.

In Source 3 de Valera, in an explanation to an American friend following the signing of the Anglo-Irish Treaty, states that he had put the external association proposal to the Dáil Cabinet and no objections had been raised. De Valera had made the proposal following his return from a series of meetings with Lloyd George in London in July 1921. What followed was a flow of correspondence between London and Dublin, which eventually established the framework for the formal negotiations that opened on 11 October. The Irish delegation negotiated on the basis of external association, but not all of the delegates were committed to the principle, or even understood the significance of the unique constitutional concept developed by de Valera. In formulating the external association proposal de Valera had a number of objectives. His meetings with Lloyd George had confirmed that the British would not accept Ireland becoming a republic and would even refuse to enter negotiations if full independence for Ireland was on the table. In these circumstances de Valera was desperately trying to build a bridge between Irish republicanism and membership of the British Commonwealth. As Source 3 explains, external association would not have compromised Irish independence and would have given Ireland a constitutional link with the nations of the British Commonwealth. However, the Sinn Féin leader was fully aware that the Coalition government would not tolerate Ireland becoming an 'external associate' of the Commonwealth, but he also sought to use the device of external association to maintain a fragile unity in his Dáil Cabinet. In particular, he needed to retain the support of hardline republicans such as Brugha, Stack and Childers, who were opposed to Irish membership of the Commonwealth. While the concept of external association actually foreshadowed the constitutional arrangements that evolved between countries like India and the Commonwealth after the Second World War, the notion that a country could be a republic and a member of the Commonwealth was unacceptable in 1921. In Source 3 de Valera also attempts to justify his actions during the period of the Treaty negotiations. His reference to the Dáil Cabinet's support for external association fails either to highlight the lack of commitment to the concept among some of the delegates or, more significantly, to admit that his meetings with Lloyd George in July had confirmed that Britain would only accept membership of, not association with, the Empire. Furthermore, the letter to McGarrity also defends de Valera's refusal to attend the negotiations, claiming that the Irish delegation agreed with his view and had been given a draft Treaty, containing the external association proposals, "to guide them". For the British, however, external association meant a republic, and they were determined to prevent this, even if it meant military intervention.

Source 1 reinforces the idea that external association was never a viable option during the Treaty negotiations. The insistence that "loyalty to the Throne and Empire" should be at the core of any treaty with Sinn Féin ruled out the prospect of external association even receiving serious consideration. Moreover, Lloyd George's belief that public opinion in Britain was solidly behind such a stance ensured that the British delegation would not deviate from this commitment during the negotiations. Indeed, the Prime Minister's view that public opinion in Britain would support the reopening of the military campaign in Ireland, if the Irish refused to accept loyalty to the Crown and membership of the Empire, enabled Lloyd George to use the threat of war to push the Irish delegation towards the acceptance of dominion status. As the British prepared for the beginning of negotiations, therefore, they were determined that if the conference broke down it should do so on the refusal to accept the Crown and Empire, because this would allow the Coalition government to occupy the moral high ground and unite public opinion. This strategy spelt doom for de Valera's external association concept. Yet Source 1 also acknowledges that Ulster would present a major obstacle to British objectives during the Treaty negotiations. The Lloyd George government recognised that the Irish delegation would use the existence of partition to cloud the issue on national status, and that Irish acceptance of the Crown and Empire might be conditional on securing the unity of Ireland, but the proposal of a Boundary Commission saw the Prime Minister negotiate this particular difficulty. The other key factor which made it impossible for Lloyd George to consider external association was his dependence on Conservative support to keep the Coalition government in power. Any settlement that left Ireland outside the Empire would have been unacceptable to the Conservatives and their leaders, Chamberlain and Birkenhead, both of whom were prominent figures in the British delegation.

Source 2 suggests that some members of the Irish delegation still thought that the British would make concessions on the Crown and Empire issues as the negotiations neared conclusion. By this stage, as Source 2 illustrates, splits both within the Irish negotiating team and the Dáil Cabinet had deepened. Most attention was focused on the oath of allegiance. However, room for manoeuvre was limited as the British had flatly rejected the Irish proposal for external association, which had been presented to the British in draft form towards the end of November. By this stage of the negotiations it was clear that symbolism had become very important to both sides, but the British refused to budge on the issues of Crown and Empire. Still, on their return to London following the dramatic meeting of the Dáil Cabinet on 3 December, Barton, Duffy and Childers once again attempted to press the case for external association. They were rebuffed by indignant British delegates who now prepared for a breakdown of the conference and a possible return to war. Significantly, Griffith and Collins, the two dominant figures in the Irish delegation, had concluded that external association would not be accepted by the British, and neither was prepared to risk war over the issue. Therefore, while part of the Irish delegation continued to demand external association right up to the end of the negotiations, the British delegation was united in its determination to ensure that Ireland accepted dominion status within the Empire and, if necessary, was prepared to make this an issue of war. As Source 2 demonstrates, the split within the Irish delegation also meant that the case for external association was not made as effectively as it might have been.

While Source 3 suggests that external association was a viable concept for the Irish delegation to pursue, Sources 1 and 2 show that such a course was doomed to fail.

Q3

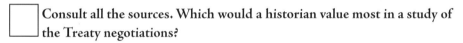 **Consult all the sources. Which would a historian value most in a study of the Treaty negotiations?**

Each of these sources provides useful evidence to a historian studying the making of the Anglo-Irish Treaty.

Source 1, an extract from George Boyce's book on the Lloyd George government's Irish policy, summarises the strengths and weaknesses of the British position on the eve of the negotiations. The source is particularly useful, because it throws light on the careful preparations made by the British government leading into the negotiations. It also describes the care with which the British considered the influence of public opinion. Lloyd George and his colleagues were sure that they could make specific demands on the Crown and Empire, as this would "command universal acceptance" from the British people. Crucially, Source 1 refers to the confidence of the British delegation in the anticipated support for renewed military engagement, if the Sinn Féin representatives refused to accept the oath of allegiance and membership of the Commonwealth. The source also highlights the great disadvantage facing the British as they entered negotiations. The British delegates knew that Sinn Féin would seek to exploit the border question, and they were pragmatic enough to sense that Ulster was not an issue on which they could consider any reopening of the war. Public opinion in Britain would not tolerate such a course of action. The passage states clearly that the public was very likely to support a war to defend partition. It specifically raises the future of Tyrone and Fermanagh, the two counties in the new Northern Ireland state that had Nationalist majorities, because Lloyd George knew that if the conference broke down on this issue, it would leave his Coalition government in a very difficult position. Significantly, Source 1 implies that the Prime Minister could not expect practical assistance from Craig's embryonic administration in Belfast if he came under pressure from the Irish delegation on the border question during the negotiations. Indeed, it was only Lloyd George's skilful use of the Boundary Commission concept that enabled him to derail the Sinn Féin plan to make concessions on the Crown and Empire conditional on the enhanced prospects for a United Ireland. Boyce's work goes on to emphasise the quality of a British delegation that included Lloyd George, Chamberlain, Birkenhead and Churchill and their shrewd understanding of their Irish opponents. These were able and experienced negotiators who knew how to maximise their advantages and overcome their weaknesses. Therefore, Source 1 accurately describes a British team that was focused, prepared and united in its objectives, and one that had learnt to pay closer attention to public support for the government's Irish policy following the disaster of the War of Independence.

In Source 2 the historian Arthur Mitchell describes the difficulties confronting the Irish delegation as the negotiations reached a climax, and he captures the drama of the highly-charged meeting of the Dáil Cabinet on Saturday, 3 December 1921. Tension boiled over when Brugha launched a stinging personal attack on Griffith and Collins – the two dominant figures on the Irish delegation who had participated in sub-conferences with their British counterparts. Brugha was alleging that the British had suggested the sub-conference method, and had deliberately chosen to negotiate with Griffith and Collins because they recognised that these two were the most likely to accept the Crown and Empire in a new constitutional arrangement. Yet the use of sub-conferences had been a practical way of accelerating the negotiating process and, as Source 2 clarifies, it had been done with "the approval of the whole Delegation". Indeed, de Valera had been unperturbed by the development when the issue had been raised by an anxious Duffy. From the British perspective, however, the use of the sub-conference method of negotiation had enabled them to overcome a significant problem. This was because Childers, the hardline republican secretary to the Irish delegation, was sidelined – a manoeuvre which, of course, worked to the advantage of Griffith and Collins. In addition, Source 2 highlights the importance of the oath of allegiance in the Cabinet discussions. It was this single issue that really preoccupied the Sinn Féin leaders, and loyalty to the Crown was inextricably linked with membership of the Empire. At the meeting de Valera ignored the obvious division within the Cabinet, as he tried to find a form of words that would emphasise Ireland's freedom, while recognising the Crown as head of the Commonwealth. While other important issues such as trade, finance and defence had been settled, Source 2 stresses that symbols were just as important to the Irish as they were to the British. The other point of contention raised in Source 2 was Ulster, as both de Valera and Brugha objected to the clauses relating to the border. It is difficult, however, to escape from the view that the Dáil Cabinet still regarded Ulster as part of a negotiating strategy. De Valera's Document No. 2 actually included the Boundary Commission proposals, and made the oath of allegiance and dominion status the key points of difference with the Treaty. Source 2 is also useful because it reveals Collins's pragmatic nature. While he clearly did not like the wording of the oath, he was prepared to use the twelve-month interval to see "how it would work". Collins hoped that the Treaty would give Ireland the freedom to achieve freedom, and the Irish people would quickly come to appreciate this. More particularly, Collins wanted to use this period to prepare a new constitution, as required by the Treaty, which would nudge the Irish Free State towards greater freedom from Britain. Source 2 is very useful, as it describes the deep divisions within the contemporary Sinn Féin movement and focuses on the importance of the oath of allegiance.

Source 3, de Valera's letter to his American confidant Joseph McGarrity, is an important document, as it illustrates the attempts made by the Sinn Féin leader to justify his opposition to the Treaty. The signing of the Treaty on 6 December 1921 had come as a shock to de Valera, and it ruined his strategy of preserving unity within the Sinn Féin ranks. The letter explains how de Valera expected his colleagues to negotiate a Treaty on the basis of external association, and he later argued that when informed that agreement had been reached he assumed that external association had been achieved. He tells McGarrity that his new proposal for Ireland to become an external associate of the Empire had been made following his abortive talks with Lloyd George in July, when he was left in no doubt that a republic would be totally unacceptable to the British. The device of external association had been useful to de Valera in keeping Brugha and Stack, two of the doctrinaire republicans in the Dáil Cabinet, in line. He used it as the rallying ground for opponents of the Treaty following the delegation's return from London. Yet Source 3 shows no appreciation of British attitudes during the negotiations. Lloyd George led a Coalition government dominated by Conservatives, for whom the symbols of Crown and Empire were of fundamental importance. Source 3 also includes one of the reasons given by de Valera for his non-attendance at the negotiations. The Irish leader claimed that, as president of the Republic and head of state, he should never be placed in a position which may have compromised his

163

office. Yet, whatever his reasons, de Valera's failure to lead the Irish delegation meant that he lost control of events, and, as PS O'Hegarty has argued, it was his "wounded vanity" that led him to oppose the Treaty. Ronan Fanning later developed that theme by claiming that de Valera opposed the Treaty not because "it was a compromise but because it was not his compromise". De Valera's anticipation of "tricks" from Lloyd George was surely another compelling reason for his attendance. By the time he wrote to McGarrity, an influential Sinn Féin supporter in Philadelphia, de Valera was desperately trying to build support for an attack on the Treaty. Source 3 is also useful because it reveals the anger felt by de Valera at Griffith's breach of faith when promising to submit the results of the final negotiating session to the Dáil Cabinet. This would have allowed de Valera to intervene at the crucial moment, but the British exploited the confusion over the plenipotentiary status of the Irish delegates, and de Valera's plans were defeated. The letter contains an undertone of bitterness at the bad faith shown by Griffith and Collins, and its articulation of the external association concept and justification for de Valera's refusal to lead the Irish team make it a valuable document.

Each source is useful for the historian studying the Anglo-Irish Treaty. However, Source 1, with its honest assessment of British strengths and weaknesses and its analysis of Sinn Féin's probable negotiating strategy, is the most useful.

CAUSES OF THE IRISH CIVIL WAR

Source 1

Declaring that if they accepted the Treaty, they were putting two very definite barriers in the way of achieving freedom, Mr. de Valera declared one barrier would be that they were pledging the nation's honour to a certain agreement. Another barrier, if an Irish Government was set up, those who wanted to travel on the road to achieve freedom, such as those men present with the rifles, would have in the future not merely the foreign soldiers to meet, but would have to meet the force of their own brothers, their fellow country-men, who would be supporting the Government.

'Therefore, in future', he went on, 'in order to achieve freedom, if our Volunteers continue, and I hope they will continue until the goal is reached, – *if we continue on that movement which was begun when the Volunteers were started, and we suppose this Treaty is ratified by your votes, then these men, in order to achieve freedom, will have, I said yesterday, to march over the dead bodies of their own brothers. They will have to wade through Irish blood … The people had never a right to do wrong.'* He was certain that the same pluck which had carried them so far would enable them to finish.

Extract from a report published in the Irish press, 20 March 1922
Tim Pat Coogan, *De Valera: Long Fellow, Long Shadow*
(Hutchinson, Random House, 1993)

Source 2

Now this Provisional [Free State] Government is greatly strengthened. It is armed with the declared will of the Irish electorate. It is supported by an effective Parliamentary majority. It is its duty to give effect to the Treaty in the letter and in the spirit … to give full effect to it without delay. A much stricter reckoning must rule henceforward. The ambiguous position of the so-called Irish Republican Army, intermingled as it is with the Free State troops, is an affront to the Treaty. The presence in Dublin, in violent occupation of the Four Courts, of a band of men styling themselves the Headquarters or the Republican Executive, is a gross breach and defiance of the Treaty. From this nest of anarchy and treason, not only to the British crown, but to the Irish

---

people, murderous outrages are stimulated and encouraged, not only in the 26 counties, not only in the territory of the Northern Government, but even, it seems most probable, here across the Channel in Great Britain ... The time has come when it is not unfair, not premature and not impatient for us to make to this strengthened Irish Government and new Irish Parliament a request, in express terms, that this sort of thing must come to an end. If it does not come to an end, if either from weakness, from want of courage, or for some other even less creditable reasons, it is not brought to an end and a very speedy end, then it is my duty to say, on behalf of His Majesty's Government, that we shall regard the Treaty as having been formally violated.

Extract from Winston Churchill's speech to the House of Commons, 26 June 1922
HC Deb 5th series, vol 155

Source 3

The Treaty's signing was the decisive event which led to the Civil War. No document could have more effectively brought out into the open divisions in the philosophy and leadership of the Sinn Féin movement. If it had offered a little more or a little less, it may well have unified opinion for or against it. Moreover, the terms demonstrated profound differences of attitude between general opinion within the Twenty-Six Counties and the political and military leadership of the nationalist movement. The ensuing developments fully revealed the lack of effective relations between the various nationalist institutions which prevented any controlled, disciplined response to the Treaty ...

The popular support for the Treaty, however, was somewhat ambivalent. There was clearly a great desire for peace and normality and a strong feeling that the terms offered were the best that could be expected.

From Michael Hopkinson, *Green Against Green: The Irish Civil War* (Gill and Macmillan, 1988)

Q1

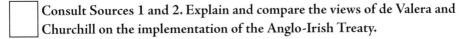

Consult Sources 1 and 2. Explain and compare the views of de Valera and Churchill on the implementation of the Anglo-Irish Treaty.

In Source 1 de Valera confirms his outright opposition to the Treaty that had been signed by the Irish and British delegations more than three months earlier. His objection is based on the promise that the Treaty, if accepted, will be an obstacle to Irish freedom. De Valera's view is that it would be dishonourable for the Irish to implement the Treaty, and he warns that such a course will lead to conflict. He urges the anti-Treaty IRA, or Irregulars as they became known, to continue the fight for Irish freedom which would mean, in effect, the rejection of the Treaty. In his call for the use of force, de Valera issues the chilling statement that the opponents of the Treaty should be prepared "to wade through Irish blood" in their struggle to uphold the virtues of the republic. By this point, of course, the Dáil had declared its support for the Treaty and had voted to remove de Valera from his position as president, replacing him with Arthur Griffith who had been the leader of the Irish delegation during the Treaty negotiations. In his attempt to rally opposition to the Treaty de Valera had issued Document No. 2, his alternative to the Treaty. Once he had emerged from his initial shock at the signing of the document, he became determined, as Source 1 illustrates, to carry the fight to his pro-Treaty opponents. Furthermore, de Valera was keen to unite the various anti-Treaty elements under his leadership, and this speech is just one example of his efforts to appeal to republican militants. He rejected Collins's stepping-stone thesis, suggesting that such a pragmatic approach would only undermine the declared principles of Irish freedom. Therefore, Source 1 reveals the dogmatic nature of contemporary Irish republicanism, which was unsuited to the politics of compromise and consensus. De Valera is insistent that the Treaty cannot be implemented even though he expected it to be endorsed by a majority of the Irish people at a forthcoming general election, something which he desperately wanted to avoid. Indeed, the uncompromising language that he uses in Source 1 can be viewed as a warning to the Provisional Government to postpone indefinitely its plans for a general election. His famous pronouncement that "The people had never a right to do wrong" is clear evidence that on the issue of the implementation of the Treaty de Valera was prepared to advance the argument that devotion to the republic ought to be sacrosanct, outweighing normal democratic convention. Not surprisingly, this statement provoked a howl of protest from the press and the Catholic Church, but it demonstrates de Valera's willingness to threaten violence in order to prevent the implementation of the Treaty.

Source 2 presents Churchill's views on the implementation of the Treaty. As Secretary of State for the Colonies, Churchill had direct responsibility for Irish affairs, and his key role as a member of the British delegation during the Treaty negotiations only reinforced his determination to see the Treaty implemented in full. Yet, as a number of historians such as Paul Canning have noted, Churchill's conduct during these critical months after the Treaty was characterised by patience and restraint, qualities he did not always exhibit in his handling of Anglo-Irish relations. Although Churchill had made allowances for the Provisional Government's problems during this period, his frustration at Collins's reluctance to adhere to his obligations under the Treaty had increased significantly towards the end of June 1922. This speech to the House of Commons came only four days after Sir Henry Wilson's assassination in London, and Churchill was putting the blame squarely on anti-Treaty elements. In the speech he demands that the authorities in Dublin take a tough line with the opponents of the Treaty, who are intent on causing mayhem and lawlessness. By this stage, Churchill argues, the Provisional Government is in a much stronger position to tackle the dissidents, because the general election on 16 June has given Collins and his ministers a clear mandate "to give effect to the Treaty". In the election to the Third Dáil, pro-Treaty candidates had received almost twice as many votes as their anti-Treaty opponents, thereby delivering the verdict that de Valera had feared in Source 1.

There is an obvious feeling in Churchill's speech that Collins had been dragging his feet on the implementation of the Treaty. This view had been endorsed by Collins's willingness to accept an electoral pact with de Valera, but Collins had believed that such a pact was essential if the election was to proceed without violence. Now that the public had had its say, however, Churchill is adamant that the Treaty should be implemented "without delay". Churchill goes on to express the Coalition government's outrage at the actions of Rory O'Connor and his militant republican supporters who had occupied the Four Courts in Dublin since 14 April, a move which he regards as "an affront to the Treaty". As Source 2 demonstrates, Churchill held O'Connor and the Republican Executive responsible for the Wilson murder, and he is convinced that the time has now come for the Provisional Government to act against these republican die-hards and assert its authority. Only prompt and decisive action can allow the Treaty to be implemented. Moreover, Churchill is keen to demonstrate that Westminster's demand for action is neither "unfair" nor "premature", especially when the strengthened position of the Provisional Government is taken into account. Churchill concludes his speech by reminding the government in Dublin of its formal obligation to adhere to the terms of the Treaty. Failure to meet the challenge of the anti-Treaty IRA, he explains, will be taken by the Westminster government as an indication that the Treaty has been "formally violated".

Therefore, Sources 1 and 2 present very different attitudes to the implementation of the Treaty, although both recognise that the precise future of the Treaty has yet to be determined.

Q2

Consult all the sources. How far do they suggest that the outbreak of the Civil War was due solely to differences over the Anglo-Irish Treaty?

All three sources suggest that the Treaty was a fundamental cause of the Irish Civil War, although Source 3 also emphasises the role played by longstanding divisions within the republican movement.

In Source 1 de Valera focuses exclusively on the Treaty, arguing that it has divided the Irish people. He warns that if the Treaty is implemented its opponents, over whom he is seeking to assert his authority, will be obliged to take up arms against "their fellow country-men". Indeed, he himself feels so strongly about the Treaty that he would encourage his followers "to march over the dead bodies of their own brothers" in a future civil war. De Valera rejected the Treaty because he regarded it as a major obstacle to Irish freedom. Should the Treaty be endorsed by popular opinion at a general election, he still insists that conflict will be inevitable, as the Irregulars will never accept an arrangement that denies Ireland its full freedom, even if it means having "to wade through Irish blood". For de Valera, therefore, the Treaty was the issue that divided Irishmen and, if implemented, would lead to civil war. Yet his insistence that further violence must be used to complete the work begun in 1916 reveals the uncompromising style of contemporary Irish republicanism, and this was undoubtedly a factor in the outbreak of the Civil War. In Joe Lee's phrase, the Civil War was a struggle between "majority right and divine right", and, as Source 1 indicates, de Valera had no scruples about ignoring popular support for the Treaty. His statement also hints at the fierce personal rivalry that had recently developed within the Sinn Féin movement. Although not a significant cause, tension between a number of republican leaders, notably Collins and de Valera, did play some part in the outbreak of civil war.

Churchill's speech points to the pivotal role played by the Treaty in the run-up to civil war. He notes that the Provisional Government has been stalling on the implementation of the Treaty in its attempts to avoid conflict, but argues that in the changed circumstances following the election of the Third Dáil the Provisional Government must fulfil its obligations and implement the Treaty. In his demand that Collins should face down his opponents, Churchill is acknowledging the fact that it is the Treaty that has provoked the split with the republican die-hards. It was their outright opposition to the Treaty that had led O'Connor and his militant supporters to occupy the Four Courts in April. Churchill claims that their action is "a gross breach and defiance of the Treaty", which was, of course, precisely what O'Connor had intended. Churchill's reference to the Republican Executive is, moreover, a warning that if the Provisional Government failed to take prompt action then dictatorship would triumph over democracy, as the expressed will of the Irish people would be cast aside. Furthermore, Churchill's angry call for the Provisional Government to assert its authority and deal with the "anarchy" in its jurisdiction reveals the extent of the pressure being exerted by the British government. While Churchill recognised the importance of the Treaty in dividing the republican movement, his demand for a strike against the republican militants, something that clearly had become a matter of real urgency following Wilson's assassination, demonstrates that the Treaty was not the sole cause of civil war. Source 2 closes with a veiled threat which highlights the importance of British pressure as a cause of the conflict. Failure to deal with the dissidents meant, in Churchill's words, that the British government would "regard the Treaty as having been formally violated". This would inevitably lead to British intervention, a development that Collins was desperate to avoid, as Churchill moved to ensure the implementation of the Treaty. Therefore, British pressure and the fear of renewed British military involvement in Ireland were important reasons for the beginning of the Civil War.

Source 3 makes the unequivocal statement that the signing of the Treaty was "the decisive event which led to the Civil War", but Hopkinson goes on to emphasise the importance of the longstanding divisions within Sinn Féin. He argues that the real significance of the Treaty was that it brought these divisions "out into the open". Yet Source 3 places the Treaty at the heart of the conflict by suggesting that if it had contained just a few more concessions much more enthusiastic support would have followed. However, it is difficult to reconcile this view with the uncompromising stance taken by O'Connor and the die-hards who were unwilling to accept any compromise on the position of the republic. Similarly, Hopkinson explains that fewer concessions to Sinn Féin in the Treaty would have united opinion against it. It was the ambiguous nature of the Treaty, therefore, that divided opinion in a way that created a significant minority. Moreover, Hopkinson questions the level of support for the Treaty, which was addressed in Sources 1 and 2, by claiming that popular support for the Treaty was "somewhat ambivalent". He argues that war weariness among the Irish people had reinforced the desire for "peace and normality", and he credits the electorate with a profound sense of realpolitik, as they appreciated that the concessions gained by the Irish negotiating team were "the best that could be expected". Of course, implicit in Hopkinson's argument, citing the Treaty as the main cause of the Civil War, is his contention that the disjointed nature of the republican movement had prevented a "controlled, disciplined response to the Treaty", and this was clearly a major contributor to the Civil War. Sinn Féin had emerged in 1917 as an umbrella movement catering for many shades of Nationalist opinion. Key philosophical differences, to which Source 3 refers, had been buried rather than resolved as the struggle against the British in the War of Independence had created a pragmatic unity. Furthermore, the evolution of a military strategy in which local warlords used guerrilla warfare to engage the British, permitted the development of a movement that was often resentful of attempts to control and direct it. This ensured that the IRA's response to the Treaty was often determined by personal and local considerations, and it was the failure of the republican movement to prevent this military split that became a major cause of the Civil War. Hopkinson also hints at the personal rivalry among the movement's leaders, and once again, the Treaty was the catalyst for allowing such bitter rivalry to surface. This made it difficult for the key players to resolve their differences peacefully. While Source 3 highlights the central role played by the Treaty in the outbreak of the Civil War, it also emphasises more fundamental problems that existed within the Sinn Féin movement, which made some kind of split very likely.

All of the sources examine the significance of the Treaty in the republican split, but Source 1 is the most definite in declaring that the Treaty was the sole cause of the Irish Civil War.

Q3

Consult all the sources. Which of them would a historian value most as historical evidence in a study of the causes of the Irish Civil War?

Taken together the three sources would help the historian construct a fairly detailed background to the outbreak of the Civil War.

Source 1 is a useful document as it highlights de Valera's determination to prevent the implementation of the Treaty. At this point he was seeking to undermine Collins's stepping-stone thesis, and this statement demonstrates that he would be prepared to engage in the slaughter of civil war in order to save the nation's honour. His assertion that "people had never a right to do wrong" reveals de Valera's contempt for the principle of majority rule in this instance. This is clear evidence of the dogmatic nature of contemporary Irish republicanism, which had difficulty making the transition from the military, or quasi-military, to the political stage. As the movement's sharpest political brain, de Valera had a duty to look harder for a political accommodation rather than threaten civil war, even though he felt betrayed by the signatories of the Treaty. De Valera, of course, went on to enjoy a long and distinguished political career, but most historians are agreed that this period in the run-up to the Civil War was his 'darkest hour', and there is evidence in Source 1 to endorse this viewpoint. In his defence it can be argued that de Valera was still fumbling to find a suitable response to the London agreement and the subsequent

171

actions of the Provisional Government. Unlike O'Connor and the die-hards, he was concerned to articulate the anti-Treaty position and assert his authority over the opponents of the Treaty, at least in a political sense. Still, the deliberate use of provocative phrases, such as wading through Irish blood and marching over the dead bodies of brothers, was irresponsible and probably encouraged the more excitable young men to take up arms. Even though de Valera subsequently attempted to withdraw these comments, they were naturally seized upon by the press and can only have deepened the divisions among Irish people over the Treaty. In particular, the historian looking at the causes of the Civil War will be struck by the dismissal of the electorate's verdict on the Treaty, illustrating the view that a civil war would be necessary in order for Ireland to attain its freedom.

Source 2 gives the British government's view of what it regarded as the deteriorating situation in Ireland towards the end of June 1922. For a historian studying the causes of the Civil War it throws light on the role played by Churchill in the days prior to the outbreak of the conflict. He is outraged by Collins's failure to meet the challenge thrown down by O'Connor and the Republican Executive who are occupying the Four Courts in defiance of the Provisional Government. With tension increasing Churchill is accusing the militants of using their "nest of anarchy and treason" to spread violence and murder in both parts of Ireland and in England. The date of Churchill's speech is significant. Coming only a few days after Wilson's assassination, Churchill is increasing the pressure on the Provisional Government, insisting that it must "give effect to the Treaty in the letter and in the spirit" now that it has received a mandate from the Irish people. The speech also draws attention to the split, or "ambiguous position", in the IRA which was to be a crucial issue in the causes of the Civil War. His plea that the Coalition government's request for action is neither "premature" nor "impatient" highlights the restraint of the administration in London, as it controlled its frustration at the Provisional Government's tardy implementation of the Treaty. Ultimately, Churchill's warning about the violation of the Treaty carried a threat which Collins and his colleagues could not ignore. By this stage, the Provisional Government realised that if it continued to delay an attack on the Four Courts occupants it risked British intervention. Indeed, Churchill was moving towards the issue of an ultimatum to the Provisional Government, and Source 2 clarifies the final stages of this journey. When the Civil War did begin only days after the Churchill speech, the British were to demonstrate their support for the Provisional Government by supplying weapons and artillery. The real value of Source 2 for the historian studying the causes of the Civil War is its emphasis on the role played by British government pressure as an immediate cause of the conflict.

Source 3 stresses the significance of the Treaty as the "decisive event" leading to the Civil War. Hopkinson explains that the real significance of the Treaty was its role in exposing the serious divisions that already blighted the Sinn Féin movement. Hitherto, those divisions, which had centred on both the "philosophy" and the "leadership" of the movement, had been concealed as all its elements – military and political – had been united in the revolutionary struggle against British rule. Source 3 demonstrates how the signing of the Treaty, and the confusion it generated, brought these differences to the surface, and this was a crucial factor in the outbreak of the Civil War. Hopkinson also highlights the gap between the people and the republican leadership, a development alluded to in Sources 1 and 2, as a self-appointed revolutionary elite contemptuously ignored popular opinion and prepared to defend republican purity in a civil war. The reference to philosophical differences is underlined by Collins's view of the Treaty as a stepping stone to independence, and the rejection of this argument by de Valera and the more militant O'Connor, who believed that it was an obstacle to Irish freedom. Within the leadership, moreover, bitter personal rivalry had emerged even before the end of the War of Independence. Hopkinson links the "lack of effective relations between the various nationalist institutions" to the Treaty in his claim that these competing elements ensured opinion would be divided. This was especially true of the IRA, as its response to the Treaty was primarily determined by geography, social class and personal loyalty. The author, who is an acknowledged expert on both the IRA and the Civil War, later demonstrates the way in which this military split led directly to civil war. Finally, Hopkinson offers a shrewd perspective on public support for the Treaty, hinting that it was lukewarm in many areas, particularly in the more prosperous east of the country where there was a real desire for a return to "normality" after the violence and upheaval of the War of Independence. This would suggest that the general election results, to which Churchill attached great significance in Source 2, may not have been as clear-cut as they appeared on the surface. Furthermore, the comment on the electorate's view that the Treaty, while disappointing, offered the "best" deal available in the circumstances, may be a testament to the power of the press which was clearly pro-Treaty. It certainly supports the opinion that political consciousness was well developed among the Irish electorate, exposing the misplaced judgement demonstrated by de Valera in Source 1.

Each of the three sources sheds valuable light on the causes of the Civil War. Source 1 highlights republican dogmatism and de Valera's personal commitment to violent opposition to the Treaty, while Source 2 illustrates the crucial role played by British pressure in the days before the outbreak of the conflict. However, Source 3 is the most valuable, as it unravels the link between the Treaty and the opening of hostilities, demonstrating how this exposed serious tensions within the greater republican movement. Moreover, it offers a perceptive analysis of the electorate's view of the Treaty and highlights the gap that existed between this pragmatic approach and the vision of the republican idealists.

PARTITION

Source 1

United Irish League
39 Upper O'Connell Street,
Dublin,
13th February, 1920.

My dear Lord Bishop,

I am crossing to-night to London and I would be very glad to hear from you on the situation. As far as I can see the situation, it means that a Parliament will be set up in the North of Ireland, and I am practically certain not for the whole of Ulster but for the Six Counties. It is then likely they will proceed to put the Bill into operation in that portion of Ireland that wants it, and that Carson will establish his Parliament for the Six Counties.

This will mean the worst form of partition and of course permanent partition. Once they have their own Parliament with all the machinery of government and administration, I am afraid anything like subsequent union will be rendered impossible. I propose if an opportunity is offered to attack the Bill, and to do so from an Ulster point of view giving reasons why we Catholics and Nationalists could not under any circumstances consent to be placed under the denomination [sic] of a Parliament so skilfully established as to make it impossible for us to be ever other than a permanent minority, with all the sufferings and tyranny of the present day continued, only in a worse form.

Letter from Joe Devlin to Bishop Patrick O'Donnell of Raphoe
ADA Patrick O'Donnell Papers, IV, 5

Source 2

We would much prefer to remain part and parcel of the United Kingdom ... But we have many enemies in this country, and we feel that an Ulster without a parliament of its own would not be in nearly as strong a position as one in which a parliament had been set up, where the executive had been appointed and where above all the paraphernalia of government was already in existence ... We do not know how long, if we did not take a parliament, our Unionist friends in this country could hold the fort against the forces which would be brought to bear on them, and we know that attempts on our liberty would be repeated time and again, and therefore I say that we prefer to have a parliament, although we do not want one of our own ...

We quite frankly admit that we cannot hold the nine counties ...
Sinn Féiners ... could make it impossible for us to govern those three counties [Cavan, Donegal, Monaghan] ...

Extract from Charles Craig's speech to the House of Commons, 20 March 1920
HC Deb 5th series, vol 127

Source 3

Craig ... secured in 1921 the six county area which he and Carson had sought since 1914. The unionists also secured the division in two of nearly all Irish government services and ensured that the Northern Irish senate, unlike that planned for the south, would not be weighted in favour of the minority. They lost other battles. The establishment of a council of Ireland which would consist of equal numbers from both parliaments and would deal with matters of common interest was opposed by the unionists but they can hardly have seen its inclusion in the government's bill as a serious threat ... Far more significant was the imposition of proportional representation on both parts of Ireland ... The government saw PR as a means of protecting both minorities, protestants in the south and catholics in the north. In the south Sinn Féin declared its support for PR ... but from the very beginning, long before the 1920 election results confirmed their distaste, Craig and his followers made clear their opposition to the new system, petitioned against it, and promised they would abolish it at the first opportunity. Their pleas were rejected and the bill laid down that in both parts of Ireland elections must be held under PR for the first three years of the new parliaments' lives.

From Michael Laffan, *The Partition of Ireland 1911–25* (Dundalgan Press, 1983)

Q1

Consult Sources 1 and 2. Explain and compare the views of Devlin and Craig on the 1920 Government of Ireland Bill.

Sources 1 and 2 reveal very different attitudes to the Government of Ireland Bill.

In Source 1 Joe Devlin, the Ulster Nationalist leader, is sharing his views with Bishop O'Donnell, a leading Catholic cleric from Donegal and a close confidant of Devlin's, as he prepares to cross to London to participate in the Westminster debate on the bill. Devlin's letter shows that he suspects partition will be for six counties and not the nine counties as the Long Committee, which drafted the bill, initially wanted. He considers this the "worst form of partition", as it would place the Nationalist population of the six counties in the role of a permanent minority under a Unionist-dominated parliament in Belfast. This would mean, in effect, "permanent partition", because the Unionists would enjoy a 2:1 majority, and not the more even split of a nine-county area which would have offered the Catholic minority in the North some prospect of eventual reunification. Devlin also declares that the formation of a Belfast parliament and the establishment of a separate state apparatus would ensure that partition became a permanent feature. His reference to such a parliament being "so skilfully established" can be seen as an attack on the British government's failure to resist Unionist pressure for a more homogeneous area, guaranteeing greater security for Ulster Protestants. Of course, with the House of Commons being dominated by the Coalition Conservatives, whose sympathies were firmly with the Ulster Unionists, there was little hope of a favourable outcome in the bill for the North's minority. In these circumstances, Devlin points to a very bleak future for the Catholic minority, as they can expect to be subjected to further suffering and tyranny, "only in a worse form". Naturally, the prospect of partition represented a serious threat for Northern Catholics, and their fears of maltreatment and discrimination at the hands of their political opponents, only now with institutional backing, were genuine. Previously, Devlin's support for John Redmond had been the crucial factor in the Ulster Nationalist Convention's acceptance of six-county exclusion as part of the Lloyd George peace initiative after the Rising, but this did not involve the creation of a separate Belfast parliament, and the agreement was based on a clear understanding that the arrangement would be temporary. By 1920, however, Devlin had become a disillusioned figure who, unlike his Sinn Féin opponents, recognised the dangers for his people in the government's partition scheme. As Source 1 indicates, he clearly believes that the Catholic community in the North would be abandoned and that the Unionists would seize the opportunity presented by the British government to develop a permanent state. In considering his strategy for opposing the bill Devlin believes that the best course is to highlight the plight of the Catholic minority, ignoring, just like Sinn Féin, the parallel arrangements planned for the South. Indeed, the main opposition to the Government of Ireland Bill's passage through parliament came from Devlin and the IPP rump that had survived the Sinn Féin general election landslide in December 1918. As Sinn Féin abstained from Westminster and ignored the Government of Ireland Bill, Devlin struggled to gain a hearing for the Nationalist case and, as his letter to O'Donnell suggests, he had become defeatist in his attitude to the government's plans.

Source 2, on the other hand, presents the official Unionist view of the Government of Ireland Bill. Charles Craig, the brother of Sir James Craig and the Westminster MP for South Antrim, was a leading Ulster Unionist insider who articulated the real views of Ulster Unionists on the Government of Ireland Bill. Although Ulster Unionists could claim that they never sought a regional parliament, Source 2 demonstrates that, just as Devlin feared, they could see distinct advantages for themselves in such an arrangement. In the speech Craig argues that a devolved parliament in Belfast would act as a bulwark against future attempts by their political enemies in Britain to force them into a United Ireland. While the present Coalition government was in power, dependent as it was on Conservative support, Craig was confident that there would be no attempt to coerce Ulster Unionists against their wishes. However, he had to think of the future, when some of their "many enemies" – such as a hostile Labour or Asquith-led Liberal government – might be in power. Moreover, the Unionist leadership must have sensed that the Conservatives, while still supportive, did not share the enthusiasm for the Unionist cause that they had shown in the years prior to the First World War, when the Tory party was reeling from the effects of three general election defeats in a row. In these circumstances, Craig argues, a regional parliament would provide a safety net. Interestingly, Craig's assessment concurs with Devlin's view that the Unionist position would be strengthened once "all the paraphernalia of government" was established. Craig's reference to the six-county area clarifies the Unionist position on the territory they wanted under their jurisdiction in the bill. The nine-county option favoured by the British is firmly rejected, as the Ulstermen demanded the largest area that they could comfortably control. For Craig and his colleagues, a sectarian head-count had decided that this should be six counties, and this was their price for supporting the Government of Ireland Bill. While this brought protests from Unionists in the three excluded counties, many of whom had signed the Covenant in the previous decade, the Unionists saw six as a more stable unit. They had formally adopted this position at a meeting of the Ulster Unionist Council on 10 March 1920. Therefore, although Craig opens by declaring that Unionists would prefer direct rule from Westminster, he goes on to reveal an honest Unionist assessment of the bill.

These sources offer opposite views of the Government of Ireland Bill.

Q2

Consult all the sources. How far do they suggest that the partition proposals would create serious difficulties for the Northern minority?

Each of the sources suggests that the Government of Ireland Bill contained insufficient protection for the Catholic minority, although Source 2 makes only an indirect comment.

In Source 1 Devlin, the Ulster Nationalist leader, expresses his fears for Northern Catholics if they come under Unionist rule in a six-county state. He thinks that the creation of a six-county state, which he has learned is the likely outcome, will "mean the worst form of partition". His fear is that Catholics, if outnumbered 2:1, would suffer much worse treatment than they would in a nine-county Ulster, where they would make up almost 44 per cent of the population. Even more worrying for Devlin is his concern that a six-county bloc would make "permanent partition" much more likely, as Unionists would use their parliament and "all the machinery of government and administration" to strengthen their position. Unlike the 1912–14 period when Devlin had dismissed the prospect of Unionist resistance to Home Rule as mere bluster, his letter to O'Donnell on the eve of the bill coming before the House of Commons confirms that he now understands the Unionist mentality. A separate parliament, once established, would develop a momentum of its own with dire consequences for the Northern minority. The recipient of the letter, Bishop O'Donnell, had been a longstanding supporter of the IPP, and his particular concern was that Catholic control of education would be diluted by a Unionist government. He consistently requested that Devlin should raise the education question in any discussion of devolution at Westminster. Devlin's tactic in opposing the bill is to focus exclusively on the plight of the Northern minority, ignoring the wider provisions contained in the bill, claiming that the devolution proposals would lead to a worse predicament for Northern Catholics who are already suffering from Unionist "tyranny". His warning that the minority would find itself under the "denomination [sic]" of a Protestant parliament is an indication that Devlin would dismiss any safeguards in the bill, designed to protect Northern Catholics, as worthless.

While Source 2 does not deal directly with the prospects for the Catholic minority under a Belfast parliament, it contains a number of arguments which Devlin and his fellow Nationalists would have found objectionable. Craig's claim that a regional parliament would cement Unionist power in the North and erect a major obstacle to reunification raised concerns about the need for the protection of the Northern minority. The desire to free themselves from Westminster interference, which the speech highlights as a crucial advantage, raised the possibility of a Unionist-dominated parliament enacting legislation that disadvantaged the minority. Naturally, this meant that the Government of Ireland Bill required specific safeguards to guarantee impartiality. While Craig makes no mention of these provisions, it is clear that the regional parliament would require careful scrutiny from Westminster. Yet the tone of Craig's speech indicates that Unionists would not welcome any such attempt to influence a Belfast parliament, and Devlin and the other Nationalist MPs were unlikely to be reassured by any promises, no matter how specific. The frank admission in the speech that the Unionists could not "hold" a nine-county area is further evidence that they foresaw serious sectarian strife as the new state sought to exert its authority. Indeed, considering the deep sectarian divisions in the North, Craig's lack of concern for the Catholic minority is very informative by itself.

Unlike Sources 1 and 2, Source 3 offers details of the safeguards for the Northern minority that were contained in the provisions of the Government of Ireland Act. The legislation outlined plans for a new council of Ireland which would allow Northern and Southern representatives to discuss matters of mutual interest. In theory, this body could have provided a forum to deal with minority concerns, but this was by no means guaranteed and in any case, as Source 3 confirms, Unionists did not regard it as "a serious threat". Similarly, the Northern Ireland senate offered little protection for the Catholic minority, because, unlike the proposed second chamber in the South, it "would not be weighted in favour of the minority". The most clear-cut safeguard for the Northern minority was the imposition of PR for both local and parliamentary elections. While Sinn Féin had welcomed this in the South, Ulster Unionist opposition to the measure merely confirmed that Unionists regarded PR as a serious threat to their grip on power. They had tried to use their influence, which had guaranteed six rather than nine counties, to have PR dropped from the proposals, and threatened to abolish it "at the first opportunity". Obviously, the provision of safeguards for the Northern minority had been a matter of great concern for the Westminster authorities drafting the bill, and the decision to concede the Unionist demand for a six-county parliament should have signalled the need for much more effective safeguards for the Northern minority, a necessity confirmed by the bitter sectarian past. Yet the protection for the minority in the partition proposals was woefully inadequate. PR did guarantee fair representation for Nationalists, but it was removed for local government elections in 1922 and for Northern Ireland parliamentary elections in 1929. Only active monitoring of the regional parliament's treatment of the minority could have guaranteed equality and fairness. However, Westminster was keen to distance itself from the Ulster question by 1921, and it quickly became clear, moreover, that it depended on the Ulster Unionists to work the Government of Ireland Act.

While Source 3 outlines some of the safeguards for Northern Catholics, these proved ineffective, confirming the fears expressed by Devlin in Source 1 and the Unionists' lack of concern for the minority revealed in Source 2.

Q3

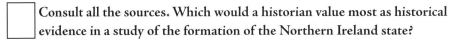

Consult all the sources. Which would a historian value most as historical evidence in a study of the formation of the Northern Ireland state?

All three sources contribute to an understanding of the formation of the Northern Ireland state.

Source 1 is a very revealing document. The letter highlights Devlin's fears of partition and of the consequences this will have for the Northern minority. At this stage in the War of Independence he grasps the real significance of partition for Irishmen. Irrespective of Sinn Féin's influence, the Coalition government will accede to Unionist demands, and by the time the republican movement sits down to discuss the future political shape of the island a newly-partitioned state in the North will be a reality. Moreover, the establishment of a separate parliament and administration will, he predicts, entrench the partition settlement, a development which will be strengthened by the Westminster decision to opt for a six-county settlement. This will strengthen the Unionist position and make things very difficult for the Catholic minority. Source 1 also provides evidence of Devlin's frustration with Sinn Féin's attitude to the proposals. By abstaining from Westminster the Sinn Féin leaders were giving their opponents a free run, and their refusal to consider devolution for the South meant that the bill would be implemented for "that portion of Ireland that wants it". Once the Unionists have their own parliament, he predicts that the minority will suffer from "the worst form of partition", as Unionist tyranny will intensify. While he rails against the injustice of partition, Devlin knows that the political situation at Westminster, where the Coalition government defers to the Conservative majority on Irish matters, means that partition is inevitable. He informs O'Donnell that he will attack the bill on the basis of institutionalised discrimination against the already beleaguered minority, but he is resigned to defeat. What made the partition proposals even more difficult for Devlin to accept was his role in persuading a majority of Ulster Catholics to accept temporary six-county exclusion during the Lloyd George peace initiative in June 1916. The Devlin letter is an invaluable document, as it provides an accurate analysis of both the government's and the Ulster Unionists' motives, while expressing genuine Nationalist fears.

Source 2 is a very useful document, because it reveals Sir James Craig's opinions about the Government of Ireland Bill. With Carson gradually withdrawing from the front line, Sir James was the effective leader of Ulster Unionism, and Charles Craig's speech succinctly sums up current Unionist thinking. While Ulster Unionists liked to describe the bill as a 'supreme sacrifice', Craig acknowledges the fundamental Unionist belief that the establishment of an Ulster parliament would make it very difficult for a future Westminster government to push Unionists into a United Ireland. Unionists were convinced that Westminster would always take the expressed wishes of that Ulster parliament into consideration. This marks a remarkable turnaround for Ulster Unionists. They had fought a determined campaign against any form of Home Rule and were now accepting just such a parliament, arguing that it offered the best protection of Protestant Ulster's future. While Craig's speech warns of the threat to Unionist security posed by their "enemies" at Westminster, particularly the emerging Labour Party, the reality was that all the main parties at Westminster had other priorities and were keen to avoid becoming bogged down in Irish affairs. Craig also confirms Devlin's fear that the prompt establishment of a separate state apparatus would have the effect of making partition permanent. In his closing remarks he focuses on the significance of a parliament for six counties, a development that his brother had played a crucial role in determining. Only four of Ulster's nine counties had Protestant majorities, but Carson and Craig had, since 1914, openly campaigned for the exclusion of six counties. The Unionist problem, articulated by Craig, was that they could not "govern" an area with such a high proportion of Catholics. Although the Coalition government recognised the significance of a nine-county area, which would increase minority representation and facilitate future reunification, a development that British ministers wanted to encourage, it buckled under Unionist pressure and agreed to a six-county bloc. The principal value of Source 2 is, therefore, its analysis of the rationale behind Ulster Unionist support for the Government of Ireland Bill.

Source 3 concentrates on an assessment of the safeguards for the Northern minority contained in the 1920 legislation. The historian Michael Laffan dismisses both the council of Ireland and the proposed Northern Ireland senate as ineffective bodies that could offer little protection for the minority community. Laffan also explains that the Coalition government insisted on the use of PR, in spite of fierce Unionist opposition, in both parts of Ireland. PR was intended to offer added protection to the Catholic minority in the North, because it meant fair representation for the Nationalist community in both local government and Northern Ireland parliamentary elections. Although Source 3 records that the Government of Ireland Act guaranteed PR in elections for a period of three years, the Unionist administration in Belfast kept its promise to abolish it at the earliest opportunity. Laffan's analysis begins with a reference to the Unionist success in securing a six-county area. Although only four counties had Protestant majorities, Ulster Unionists believed that they required a six-county area in order to make a viable state. This area was, moreover, the maximum area which they felt they could control without the fear of being outbred by Catholics – something that Unionists thought likely in a nine-county state. Another historian, Nicholas Mansergh, had previously argued that the principle of devolution and the area in question were interdependent. Mansergh argued that a nine-county excluded area would have been acceptable if direct rule from Westminster was to be implemented. If, however, a separate Ulster parliament were to be established, then a more homogeneous area was essential for Unionists to give their backing. Source 3 is a particularly useful document, because it highlights the success that partition was for the Ulster Unionists, reinforcing Ronan Fanning's contention that the Westminster government's capitulation to Ulster Unionist pressure describes the 'Ulstercentric' nature of the legislation.

While each source adds to the historian's understanding of the factors that led to the formation of the Northern Ireland state, Source 1 is the most useful. It is wide-ranging, analysing both the Catholic minority's fears and the opportunism of a triumphant Ulster Unionist Party.

Decline of the IPP

Source 1

Parliamentarianism in Ireland has reached its lowest depth, and not alone that, but the lowest depth ever reached by any Irish political movement with any popular support. It has calmly listened to a proposal for the dismemberment of Ireland and declared its willingness to accept it. In these columns last month we wrote: 'The probabilities are that the English will take advantage of the crisis in order to make a new settlement which will emphasize the division of the nation, will bring forward some scheme the operation of which will tend towards making a permanent estrangement possible'. And the English have done precisely that, have brought forward a proposal which is intended to place in their hands the means of maintaining a permanent division in this nation, of maintaining a permanent grip upon Irish soil, of still maintaining within our body politic a foreign solidity which would nullify all efforts to rebuild the nation. The subserviency and incapacity of Mr. Redmond and his Party have emboldened the English to paralyse even the petty Bill which the Government of Ireland Bill was, and to make a proposal which, if accepted, will split the Irish nation effectively, and, if not accepted, will smash the Bill and enable the Liberal Party to act the role of the injured innocent. Never in any responsible assembly was so shamefully corrupt a proposal made, and never was it so shamelessly listened to by the representatives of a nation it proposed to dismember, and never did an alleged National press so shamelessly lie about it.

Extract from an article in the *Irish Freedom*, April 1914

Source 2

Against this background [in May 1916], the Irish Party's dilemma was graphically described by Devlin who in the aftermath of the executions confided to Dillon: 'If the government had intended to add to our difficulties, they could not have selected a better means or a better time to carry out that object … the amazing thing to me is that everybody in Ireland has not been driven into the Sinn Fein movement'. He added that the country was being 'greatly and needlessly embittered' by the government's continuing policy of martial law and mass arrests which he regarded as 'entirely inexcusable'.

The Ulster Nationalist leader shared Dillon's strong view that the Irish Party must seek to turn the tide of popular indignation to its advantage by striking a more critical, independent stance at Westminster. This viewpoint, however, was rejected by Redmond who felt that any nationalist attempt to embarrass the British government in the crisis would 'lose all we have gained (in Britain) by our attitude towards the war'. Since the policy of 'marking time' was clearly fatal, there was only one alternative: the Irish leaders must somehow attempt to conjure Home Rule out of the surrounding chaos; otherwise, as T.P. O'Connor warned Dillon, 'the Irish Party is dead'.

From Eamon Phoenix, *Northern Nationalism: Nationalist Politics, Partition and the Catholic Minority in Northern Ireland 1890–1940* (Ulster Historical Foundation, 1994)

Source 3

The situation is extremely critical and very bad. The Ulstermen are more stiff and irreconcilable than they were two years ago. The Southern Unionists led by Lord Midleton have come a long way and are agreed with the Nationalists on all points but 'customs' … Redmond has, I fear, gone too far on the road of concession and is, I gather, anxious to agree with Lord Midleton … And I am convinced that if the Nationalists were to agree with the Southern Unionists and surrender the customs, in the present state of Ireland, we and the Southern Unionists would be swept off the field in a few weeks. Sinn Féin, linked with [William Martin] Murphy and the [Irish] Independent and three-quarters of the priests, would carry the country hands down … It would be the July [1916] negotiations over again in a much worse form …

Extract from a letter from John Dillon to TP O'Connor, explaining his anxiety about the Irish Convention, 10 January 1918 TCD: Dillon Papers MS 6742/435

Q1

Consult Sources 1 and 2. Explain and compare the difficulties facing the IPP in April 1914 and in May 1916.

Both sources highlight the difficulties facing the IPP at critical points in the party's history, but Source 1 is written from the perspective of one of its fiercest political opponents.

The recently launched *Irish Freedom* was a militantly separatist newspaper which articulated the views of the IRB, a revolutionary organisation that was enjoying something of a revival under the direction of Tom Clarke. The IRB had seized the opportunity presented by the formation of the Irish Volunteers in November 1913 to infiltrate mainstream Nationalism and use its influence to encourage a rising against British rule. From the outset, the *Irish Freedom* had attacked the IPP in general, and Redmond's leadership in particular, for its engagement with Britain in constitutional politics. Source 1 indicates that the IRB despised constitutional Nationalists but now argues that "Parliamentarianism in Ireland has reached its lowest depth" following Redmond's acceptance of Lloyd George's county option scheme the previous month. In accepting the "dismemberment" of Ireland, the paper warns that the British government will exploit this weakness and introduce permanent partition. In addition, the article suggests that the British will use this "permanent division" to maintain a "permanent grip" or foothold in Ireland, and this will present huge difficulties for those seeking Irish freedom. The IRB's view of constitutional Nationalism's weakness was undoubtedly coloured by the organisation's belief that the British government only responded to force, as it did with Carsonism, rather than the "subserviency and incapacity" of Redmond and the IPP. The difficulties for the IPP are exacerbated by the way it has allowed itself to be hoodwinked by the present Liberal government. If the county option scheme is rejected, then the Home Rule Bill will collapse, and if it is accepted it will mean permanent partition, with the four plantation counties nullifying "all efforts to rebuild the nation". Clearly, the breaking of the one nation principle was a serious setback for the IPP, and the article's analysis of the consequences of this decision proved remarkably accurate. However, the *Irish Freedom* represented a minority viewpoint in Ireland (hence the reference to the "alleged National press" which was effectively controlled by the IPP), and the IPP continued to enjoy the overwhelming support of the electorate. While the party could not match the dynamism and momentum of the 1880s when it first rose to political prominence, it still dominated Nationalist politics, and, as Paul Bew argues, remained untouchable at the ballot box. Yet, although the *Irish Freedom* was totally unrepresentative of mainstream

Nationalist opinion, Source 1 highlights a wider concern within Nationalism that the IPP under Redmond was consistently being outmanoeuvred by a more proactive Unionist party under Carson's leadership. Moreover, the paper warns the IPP that in conceding the exclusion of some counties, the party has made a monumental error from which it will not recover. For Redmond, on the other hand, acceptance of the county option scheme was a necessary concession to help his Liberal government friends overcome Unionist opposition, and he was confident that this would only be a temporary problem en route to the establishment of Home Rule on an all-Ireland basis.

By May 1916 Redmond had taken the gamble of supporting Britain in the war, and the Easter Rising had shaken the political structure in Ireland. While Source 1 delivers fierce criticism of the IPP from its militant republican opponents, Source 2 presents an analysis of the party's problems by the leadership immediately after the Rising. In this brief passage the historian Eamon Phoenix manages to include the views of the party's four leading figures – John Redmond, John Dillon, Joe Devlin and TP O'Connor – as they engaged in crisis management following the execution of the 1916 leaders. Devlin begins by stating that the British government has greatly added to the IPP's difficulties, suggesting that they already existed, by its policy of executions. His comment that he was amazed that the party's supporters had not already been driven into the arms of the more militant Sinn Féin movement provides evidence of the real dilemma facing the IPP "in the aftermath of the executions". Adding to Devlin's frustration at the British government's post-Rising strategy was his view that the imposition of martial law and the mass arrests of suspects, many of whom knew nothing about the Easter Rising, was feeding anti-British sentiment which was rebounding on the IPP. He fully shared Dillon's view that the party had to "turn the tide" by making a decisive stand at Westminster, where it should go on the offensive against the British government. Clearly, both Dillon and Devlin, two longstanding close friends, understood the urgency of the situation and the compelling need for decisive intervention by the IPP. TP O'Connor, the party's sole representative on the mainland who was personally close to Lloyd George, also demanded action from the party in these dire circumstances. Source 2 acknowledges O'Connor's view that unless the IPP could pull an immediate Home Rule settlement out of the "chaos", the IPP would be "dead". The party leader, Redmond, also thought that action was required, but he disagreed fundamentally with Dillon and Devlin on strategy. Indeed, such division among the party leadership at this crucial juncture could only have added to the party's difficulties and hindered an effective response. Redmond, who had always been closer to the Asquith-led governments, still saw a benefit in maintaining good relations with the government in London. Source 2 reveals that he felt the

IPP had gained advantages from its pro-war stance, and to attack the government for its handling of the Rising would risk losing this goodwill. Still, Dillon ignored Redmond's caution, and the following day delivered his stinging rebuke against the British government's policy of executions and haphazard arrests, warning that it was manufacturing Sinn Féiners in huge numbers. Dillon undoubtedly had the clearest view of the impact of the Rising, as he was present in Dublin for the duration, and he was an eyewitness to the transformation of feeling in response to British actions.

Therefore, Source 2 outlines more serious difficulties for the IPP in May 1916, with the leadership united only in their assessment that the situation for the party had become desperate, while Source 1 provides a devastating critique of the IPP's handling of the Ulster crisis from an earlier period.

Q2

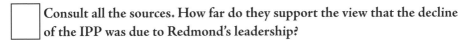
Consult all the sources. How far do they support the view that the decline of the IPP was due to Redmond's leadership?

All the sources question Redmond's leadership skills, although they do this to varying degrees.

Source 1, the extract from the *Irish Freedom*, appears to offer the most direct criticism of the IPP leader. Apart from its brief dalliance with constitutional Nationalism during the Parnell era, the IRB had consistently rejected parliamentary politics in favour of physical force. Since its launch in 1910, the paper had been a vehement critic of the IPP leader and his strict adherence to "Parliamentarianism". From the republican standpoint Home Rule fell a long way short of Irish independence, and there was a danger that such a constitutional arrangement might wean Irishmen off the desire for a full measure of freedom. The article blames "Mr. Redmond and his Party" for the shocking capitulation to the British government on the county option issue, which would allow counties to opt out of the Home Rule scheme after a plebiscite. Indeed, Redmond had played the lead role in all the Home Rule negotiations with the Liberal government, and it was his decision to accept the Lloyd George county option proposal. While one historian, AC Hepburn, has argued that Redmond used the balance of power in the House of Commons and "played a strong hand well in negotiating the parliamentary path" to a third Home Rule Bill, the *Irish Freedom* seizes on his fatal error in breaking the one-Ireland principle in March 1914. As party leader and key strategist, Redmond is blamed for presenting the English with an opportunity to divide Ireland on a permanent basis and thwart, for the foreseeable future, the efforts of those dedicated to achieving Irish freedom. Yet, in many respects, Redmond is simply a figurehead for the newspaper, as the real enemy of the IRB was constitutional Nationalism in general – any leader of the parliamentary party would have faced similar criticism. The ideology was flawed, and any leader who consorted with the British was considered an outcast. Therefore, although Source 1 specifically refers to Redmond, a man whose impeccable Westminster credentials must have irked physical-force republicans, its more general criticism was focused on the IPP and its commitment to constitutional politics.

In Source 2 Phoenix illustrates how Redmond was out of step with his lieutenants at a key moment in the party's history. By this stage the Irish leader's reputation had been seriously damaged by his support for the war, and by the War Office's bad grace, as he struggled to assert his authority over Nationalist Ireland. The IPP had become a casualty of the Easter Rising (not really a surprise considering the level of hostility directed at the IPP by the IRB in Source 1), as the insurgents targeted both constitutional Nationalism and British rule in Ireland. Source 2 confirms Redmond's mistaken view that his pro-war stance had enabled the IPP to secure significant gains and that criticism of the Asquith government would risk the loss of these gains. Yet the IPP had nothing tangible to show for its wartime support beyond Home Rule on the statute book, which Eoin MacNeill described as a "cheque post-dated". True, Redmond had been offered a Cabinet seat on the formation of the Coalition government in May 1915, but this had been declined. Clearly, the British had enjoyed all the advantages of their association with Redmond, and his reluctance to attack the policy of executions and the imposition of martial law, referred to in the passage, shows poor political judgement. Source 2 also demonstrates an air of complacency about Redmond's response to the Rising. Crucially, he did not share the sense of urgency felt by Dillon and Devlin, who were much quicker to see the consequences for the IPP of continued British coercion. Dillon, the deputy leader, sensed the immediate need to put some distance between the IPP and the government, but Redmond found it difficult to launch an attack on the British, in spite of their draconian response to the Rising. Although the party had been seriously damaged by the events of Easter 1916, a swift, unequivocal response by the leadership and an all-out attempt to influence the British government might have deflected some of the damage. Although Redmond did not create these problems and had no control over events such as the duration of the war or the IRB's decision to strike in 1916, Source 2 indicates that his pro-war stance had left him little room to manoeuvre. Furthermore, the desperate attempt "to conjure" up Home Rule led Redmond to make yet another concession to the British in the ensuing weeks, and this also backfired. That said, it is difficult to see how the IPP, even under Dillon's leadership, could have escaped its predicament in 1916.

Further evidence of tension between Redmond and Dillon appears in Source 3. The two men had never enjoyed a close relationship but had formed a very effective partnership up to 1914, when Dillon did not share Redmond's enthusiasm for the war. By January 1918 Dillon had become frustrated with Redmond's continued willingness to make concessions in an increasingly desperate attempt to secure Home Rule. His letter to TP O'Connor describes the serious dilemma facing the IPP as it struggled to reach an accommodation with Southern Unionist opinion in the Irish Convention. The Convention sat from July 1917 to May 1918 and comprised about 90 members to whom the new Prime Minister, Lloyd George, had given the responsibility of finding a workable solution to the Irish problem. By this stage, however, Sinn Féin had emerged as the dominant force in Nationalist Ireland, and it boycotted the Convention. Members were drawn from the IPP and Ulster MPs, prominent Southern Unionists and leading churchmen. During the deliberations Midleton, the Southern Unionist leader, and Redmond came close to reaching an agreement, but the Ulster Unionist deputation refused to join in the consensus. This was a last throw of the dice for an ailing Redmond, and his decision to surrender control of "customs", or fiscal autonomy as it was known, in return for Southern Unionist acceptance of Home Rule without partition caused alarm among many Nationalists.

Source 3 highlights Dillon's concern about the customs concession, describing the situation as "critical". While he recognises that the Southern Unionists have shifted their position on Home Rule, he is adamant that Redmond should resist Midleton's demand to give up customs, as this would be of crucial importance for a future Home Rule parliament. Dillon's view that this concession would finally destroy the IPP confirms the unstoppable march of Sinn Féin. He fears that Sinn Féin will be able to count on the overwhelming support of the Catholic Church, once loyal followers of the IPP. In addition, the *Irish Independent* – the newspaper founded in 1904 by William Martin Murphy, a powerful business leader and former Nationalist MP – will use its influence to support Sinn Féin's position. Clearly, an increasingly disillusioned and sceptical Dillon had kept his distance from the Convention, judging Redmond's desperate search for a settlement as too risky. His closing remark that Redmond is repeating the mistakes of the Lloyd George negotiations, only "in a much worse form", highlights his growing frustration with Redmond who died in March 1918 before the failure of the Convention. While Dillon naturally attributes some of the IPP's failings to Redmond's leadership, particularly his readiness to concede ground to the party's opponents, he recognised that the Rising and its aftermath had been the key events that undermined the IPP. In Dillon's eyes Redmond had made a series of mistakes since the outbreak of the war, and these had certainly added to the party's difficulties.

Therefore, while each source attributes blame to Redmond, particularly Sources 2 and 3, they do not provide convincing evidence that his leadership had brought about the downfall of the IPP.

Q3

Consult all the sources. Which would a historian value most as historical evidence of the decline of the IPP?

Taken together, the three sources chart the reasons for the decline of the IPP from 1914 to 1918.

Source 1 offers a republican critique of the mistake made by Redmond in March 1914. Under pressure from the Liberal government, he agreed to the county option scheme which would, in effect, have allowed the four plantation counties to opt out of the Home Rule scheme. Undoubtedly, the IPP had been damaged by this concession, and there was a general feeling that Redmond had to play second fiddle to Carson in the political crisis of 1912–14. The IRB believed this, and Source 1 records the organisation's growing disenchantment with constitutional Nationalism, citing its "subserviency" to the British government. At the same time, of course, militant Nationalists were deeply impressed by Carson's strategy of threatening force and engaging in gun running, as the Unionists sought to resist the threat of Home Rule. In Michael Laffan's phrase, "Carson had brought the gun back into Irish politics", and this proved to be a major factor in steering the IRB towards rebellion. Redmond and his colleagues would have dismissed the *Irish Freedom's* attack, as the IPP dwarfed the tiny separatist movement in 1914. However, the article is useful because it highlights very real problems for the IPP which its electoral dominance helped to conceal. Tom Garvin has described the IPP as a "hollow shell" by 1914, arguing that its strength was greatly exaggerated and that it was vulnerable to a serious challenger. In time, Sinn Féin would exploit this weakness, to which Source 1 refers, in spectacular fashion. The article is also useful because it accurately predicts the outcome of the Ulster crisis. Its warning that the "proposal for the dismemberment of Ireland" would lead to permanent partition represents a more realistic assessment of the situation than Redmond's optimistic view of all-Ireland Home Rule following a temporary adjustment. The article confirms, moreover, the IRB's withering opinion of Home Rule, which it regards as "petty", inferring that Ireland will gain no advantage whatsoever from the IPP's commitment to parliamentary politics. Finally, the reference to the party's control over the national press explains the IPP's apparent dominance in 1914, but, as Source 3 declares, there was no guarantee that such press loyalty would continue. Therefore, although Source 1 represents only the minority separatist view of constitutional Nationalism in April 1914, it highlights dangers for the IPP which Redmond and his colleagues failed to take seriously.

Source 2 is an invaluable passage, as it emphasises the dilemma facing the IPP immediately after the Easter Rising and describes the differences among the leaders. Although Devlin only mentions the impact of "martial law and mass arrests", it was these policies together with the executions that swung public opinion behind the separatists. The Ulster Nationalist leader was frustrated, because he knew that the British government was not seeking to undermine the IPP, but its actions were having this effect. While he regarded the imposition of martial law and the large number of arrests as "entirely inexcusable", his real priority, which he shared with Dillon, was to carry out a rescue mission and "turn the tide of popular indignation" by attacking the government's policy. Devlin's contact with Dillon illuminates the thinking behind Dillon's memorable attack on the government on 11 May. Indeed, Dillon's speech may have contributed to Asquith's decision to rein in the power of the military governor, General Maxwell, who had demonstrated his lack of political nous. For Dillon and Devlin, the government's failure to appreciate the fickle nature of Irish political allegiance at this crucial moment was extraordinary. As Pearse had confidently predicted, it allowed support to swing behind the insurgents and against the IPP. This passage by Phoenix indicates complacency on Redmond's part. As Bew has argued, the IPP had comfortably won all five contested by-elections in Ireland since the outbreak of the war, and this may have created a false sense of security for Redmond who, unlike Dillon, was slow to see the mood changing in Ireland. Again, Redmond's imperial loyalty, which had influenced his Woodenbridge declaration, now saw him stumble as he hesitated in attacking government policy. The failure of the party leadership to present a clear, united front at this crucial point meant that a possible opportunity to limit the damage to the IPP was lost. Source 2 concludes with TP O'Connor's simple warning that if the leaders failed to persuade the government to implement Home Rule immediately, then "the Irish party is dead". This advice proved to be correct, but in his desperation to secure Home Rule Redmond went further than he had in March 1914 by agreeing to the temporary exclusion of six counties. As Source 1 foretold, he found himself abused by a British government whose ear was attuned to Unionist voices. Therefore, Source 2 contains critical evidence of the party's problems in May 1916 and illustrates its inability to overcome these difficulties.

Source 3 reveals the depth to which the party had sunk by the beginning of 1918. Dillon's letter warns that Sinn Féin could "carry the country hands down" if Redmond makes yet another concession. Michael Laffan has noted that by the end of 1916 popular opinion in Ireland had rejected the IPP, but there was "no satisfactory alternative". By January 1918 there certainly was an alternative, and the IPP was powerless to resist its challenge. Although Sinn Féin was dismissing the IPP as an irrelevance by this stage, Redmond still clung to the hope that the imminent introduction of some form of Home Rule would enable the IPP to recover its fortunes. Hence, he engaged in the Irish Convention in what would be his final attempt to reach a *rapprochement* with Unionism. Predictably, the Ulster Unionists remained obstinate, unwilling to consider any arrangements for their protection under a Dublin parliament, but the Southern Unionists, led by Midleton, worked hard to find a consensus. While Nationalist Ireland had come to criticise Redmond for his pro-British stance in the war, this had convinced Southern Unionists that they had nothing to fear from his leadership. In his pursuit of an agreement with Midleton, however, Redmond was prepared to surrender fiscal autonomy, and Dillon's letter to O'Connor warns that this will be the final straw. Source 3 is useful because it demonstrates that, in spite of the advances made by Sinn Féin, Dillon, who was to become leader of the IPP within two months, has still not given up hope of an IPP recovery. Although his hope seemed to be without foundation, the IPP did defeat Sinn Féin in three by-elections during the next three months. Of course, these were in constituencies when the IPP had distinct advantages, and it was to prove a false dawn for the party. Source 3 also reveals the growing rift between Dillon and Redmond. Dillon had remained aloof from the Convention, indeed sharing some of Sinn Féin's disdain for the initiative, and he is clearly frustrated at Redmond's failure to learn the lesson of July 1916, where IPP concessions went unrewarded by the British government. His letter is unequivocal, warning that a further concession at this stage will see the IPP "swept off the field in a few weeks" by a dominant Sinn Féin party, which will be able to count on clerical and press support. Indeed, the withdrawal of support by both the Catholic Church and the national press, as only the *Freeman's Journal* remained loyal to the IPP, was a significant factor in the IPP's decline. Source 3 correctly speculates on the consequences of this development.

While all the sources contribute to an understanding of the decline in the IPP's fortunes, Source 2 offers the most detailed analysis of the party's difficulties, as it focuses on the problems created by the British response to the Easter Rising.